PROMISES AND PERIL

The South African Crisis

IMRAAN BUCCUS

FOREWORD BY EBRAHIM RASOOL

African perspective's

· PUBLISHING ·

African Perspectives Publishing
PO Box 95342, Grant Park 2051,
Johannesburg, South Africa
www.africanperspectives.co.za

ISBN PRINT: 978-1-0370-9531-3
ISBN DIGITAL: 978-1-0370-9532-0

Editor: Richard Gibbs
Typesetter: Phumzile Mondlani
Cover Image: Zubair Sayed
Cover Design: Jenilee Prinsloo Ryzenberg

Dedication

*With absolute gratitude to my Creator — the
source of all wisdom and strength.*

*For my beloved late parents, Mahomed (Shafy) and
Kathija Buccus; whose love shaped my world. And
taught me to face hardships with grit and grace.*

*To my selfless wife, Azeema, my anchor and
blessing and the one who steadies my heart.*

*To my daughter, Samarah, whose sharp wit, love,
and laughter fill my world with joy.*

*To my special star, Nabihah, whose unique light
teaches me new ways to see the world*

Contents

Foreword

This work by Imraan Buccus is a deceptively accessible read for any audience, especially those in the trenches for justice in a rapidly changing world. It is a compelling work that makes a robust argument for both the promise and perils facing South Africa and the world. It contains neither excessive idealism nor despair, but a realism about the challenges, while attempting to develop a toolkit that is unapologetically located on the left of the ideological spectrum, tempered by the persistent fault lines that have long beset the left.

Personally, it was a challenging read, as I was forced to reflect on my five decades of activism for justice and three decades of participation in post-apartheid governance, and the intervening years' proximity to the choices made for the transition from apartheid to democracy. Writing this foreword was cathartic. It made me face the slow unravelling of the organisation I have served for forty years, the ANC, and recall the sting of being declared persona non grata by the United States — a nation that, under Trump, yearned for the certainties of its supremacist past even as it tried to hold back the tides of global movement, technology, and change.

Yet I open myself to Buccus's challenge because a familiar life trajectory has shaped his perspective: the hardship of working-class upbringing, hard-won education, the responsibility of the activist-intellectual, and the interplay of these with persistent injustice, seeking the relevance of faith, and finding meaning and direction in ideology. He manifests a lens shaped by the dictum: When in doubt, keep left! Keeping left is premised on egalitarianism rooted in democracy — socially and economically— with participation in both elections and the everyday decisions about the details of life. It is directed at affirming dignity for all.

This lens evaluates South Africa and the world: corruption robs citizens and reduces equality; surveillance and repression inhibit freedom and accountability; violence engenders fear, and fascism feeds off such discontent; and poverty is the enemy of dignity, even if rights are abundant. As evidence, he surveys the prominent African anti-colonial and liberation movements, discerning their original instinct for the finest values worth dying for from those which made them succumb to the trappings of incumbency and power. Similarly, he embarks on a travelogue of countries where the left is evaluated to locate its vulnerability and to salvage its best practice for a world desperately in need of alternatives to the unilateralism that has bequeathed inequality, conflict, and domination.

How would the analysis, surveys, and travelogues infuse and rejuvenate a South African left, fragmented by factionalism, seduced by government office, contaminated by state capture, populated with false prophets, confused by ideological flux, and socially distanced from its popular base? Painfully, the multiple crises of the ANC are central, not so much the organisational, ideological, political, or strategic crises —

but its moral crisis! The ANC has strayed from a noble history, the values of heroic leaders, and from its popular base, because it has succumbed to avarice.

This is not a bleak read. It dissects the perils to reintroduce the reader again to the promise — a promise that emerges from global best practice, from the daily struggles of activist leaders, activism grounded in community, communities engaged in local, issue-based politics, local actions connected to a national objective, and the national contribution to the global strategy to defeat an engulfing populism that foments genocide, trade wars, and inequality.

Ebrahim Rasool

— *Ebrahim Rasool was South Africa's ambassador to the United States from 2010 to 2015, and again in 2025 under the presidency of Donald Trump. He was declared a persona non grata by President Trump and expelled for describing him as a supremicist and refusing to have South Africa withdraw its charges of genocide against Israel at the International Court of Justice (ICJ).*

Introduction

Academic writing must be presented in the language of neutrality, but it frequently stems from personal experiences. This book is about the search for justice in South Africa — and the pressing need for a rejuvenation of the country's splintered left into a viable electoral project — two issues that are deeply personal for me. I was born to a working-class family in Overport, a poor area of the port city of Durban. When I was about three or four, my father lost his job. He and his brothers decided to try their luck on a small farm on the South Coast in a rural, working-class town, about fifteen minutes south of Umzinto. The idea was to farm sugar cane, but my father knew nothing about farming. He gave it a go, and while there was some success, it was mostly a failure. Money was always tight.

There was a primary school close by and my mum sold sweets, chocolates and chips to the schoolchildren. She didn't earn much, but it made a significant difference to the family.

My father was a person people came to with problems — he could mediate, network, and find a way to help. He was also a free spirit. He'd hitchhike to Johannesburg, Lesotho or the Eastern Cape and come back with gifts or goods to sell. He'd go fishing, catch crayfish, and turn that into a little cash. This was in sharp contrast to my mother, who was careful and money conscious. They balanced each other out.

We lived in one of those "tin houses" made from wooden planks and corrugated iron. I still remember the sound of rain on that roof. Much of that world is gone now, but the house is still standing. We only got electricity when I was in Grade 10, and even then, it didn't have the kind of proper wiring you'd find in a formal house — just pipes and cables strung through. We never had running water while I was growing up.

This was sugar cane country, and the rhythms and smells of planting, burning and harvesting the cane were central. People worked themselves to the bone and stayed poor. There was a company that handled the cultivating, harvesting, and transporting of the cane to the sugar mill, taking a big cut of the profits. The real money was in owning the means of production, which we didn't.

From an early age, I started to question the myths I was told. My accounting teacher once said, "If you work like a slave, you'll live like a king." Even as a child, I knew it wasn't true. I'd seen too many people work themselves to exhaustion only to remain poor, passing that poverty to the next generation. Hard work meant little without the structures to make it count.

I first became conscious of inequality as a child, though I didn't yet have the words for it. As children, we experienced it as a strange kind of wounding. I spent most of my free time with two close friends: James, who was Black, and José, who was Portuguese and from Mozambique. We rode our bikes together, played together. We spoke fluent Zulu and never thought about race.

But on Mondays, our happy weekend bubble would burst into confusion. José would be dropped off at a well-resourced white state school in Scottburgh, dressed in a smart uniform. James would walk several kilometres to a poorly resourced Black school in an old safari-style uniform. And I went to an Indian school nearby.

Despite our existence on the margins, my primary school gave me a surprisingly good education. Thinking about my own daughter's schooling now, at a former Model C school, I realise how much care the teachers at our little working-class school put into our learning. Every morning, they'd put a copy of *The Mercury* newspaper on a table and clamp it down so it wouldn't blow away. From Grade 4 onwards, we were told to read an article and report back to the class, something that really taught us to engage with the world thoughtfully.

The newspaper was an important part of our lives. My father, who only had a primary school education himself, bought *The Mercury* every day and read it from front to back. He spent money we could barely spare on that paper. Watching him, I developed my own love for reading, and I started reading the paper at a young age.

The teachers were creative and resourceful. They labelled the trees in the area with their names, histories, and places of origin. On Arbour Day, they'd send us around to learn about the trees in the area. It was an education that extended beyond the classroom.

By the time I reached high school, I was already curious about the wider world. I had a sense of national politics from reading *The Mercury* every day, but it was still a vague, incomplete picture. Things began to take shape in Standard 6 — what's now Grade 8 — in the late 1980s. My English teacher wasn't interested in sticking to the syllabus. Instead of simply drilling us in grammar and poetry, she spoke about the African National Congress (ANC), what it stood for, and why it was banned.

At the age of 13 or so, I carried an old canvas knapsack with "Viva MK!", "Viva Apla!", and "Viva Azanla!" written across it. My English teacher noticed it and told me she'd never seen someone so young openly supporting the banned armed wing of the ANC, uMkhonto weSizwe (MK). Apla referred to the Azanian People's Liberation Army, an armed wing of the Pan Africanist Congress, and Azanla was the armed wing of the Azanian People's Organisation, the custodian of the Black Consciousness Movement. She respected my youthful daring but warned me to be careful. In retrospect, I was reckless, but at that age, I didn't quite understand the stakes.

My political understanding was maturing fast, though. A significant moment in my political development came when a new teacher, Maggie Govender, joined the school. I didn't know it then, but she was wanted by the police, working underground, and would later become a senior figure in the ANC and serve in the post-apartheid provincial government. She, along with other politically conscious teachers like KP Reddy, brought the liberation struggle into the classroom. Their influence pushed me toward underground political activity, and by 1989 — with the ANC still banned — I had joined a local branch.

My route into politics had a significant religious element. My parents emphasised the importance of religion, prayer, and morality. I valued that, but growing up as I did in the working class, I was also looking for a framework to understand poverty and racism. I wanted to know what religion had to say about oppression.

One day after the evening prayer at the local mosque, I asked the imam what Islam had to say about the way Black people were treated in this country. His face tightened with anger. He told me this was "*kufr* politics" — the politics of unbelievers — and I should focus on the Qur'an and on being a good young man. I was shocked. I respected him, but it was clear he didn't want to discuss the question.

I spoke to my father about it. He admitted he couldn't answer fully but said he had a friend who could: Fuad Hendricks, at the time the chief editor of the progressive Muslim newspaper *Al Qalam*, was warm, deeply knowledgeable, and rooted in both religion and politics. He introduced me to influential Muslim thinkers, including Ali Shariati, and reframed the understanding of the Prophet's (PBUH) life as that of a friend and defender of the poor — someone who challenged injustice directly.

Hendricks encouraged me to attend the annual Islamic Training Programme (ITP) of the Muslim Youth Movement (MYM) at As-Salaam in rural KwaZulu-Natal.

It was December 1989. There, I first heard the names Malcolm X, Sayyid Qutb and Maulana Abdul A'la Maududi — figures from around the world who had wrestled with the relationship between Islam, politics, and liberation.

I also met Na'eem Jeenah and Shamima Shaikh. Na'eem said something I had never heard before: "My spirituality is heightened when I am toyi-toying" (a powerful, protest dance characterised by high-stepping, rhythmic stomping, and synchronised chanting). I realised I felt the same — that my connection to faith was strengthened, not weakened, by standing up against oppression and being in struggle with others.

It was also at As-Salaam that I saw Ahmed Kathrada for the first time. He had just been released from 26 years in prison after being found guilty, together with Nelson Mandela and other ANC leaders, in the Rivonia Trial in 1964. Word spread that he was coming. When he exited the car, there was a guard of honour for him that toyi-toyied him all the way to the hall. When he walked in, the young people in the hall erupted into song, moving chairs aside to clear space for him. It was an electric moment. I stood next to him during the evening prayer. The moment stayed with me: a Muslim gathering, committed to faith but also to fighting apartheid, embracing a man who had spent decades behind bars for the liberation of this country.

That weekend was transformative. I had found a community of Muslims who saw no contradiction between faith and radical politics. But I also noticed the class and racial divides in the room. Some arrived in luxury German cars, immaculately dressed; others came from working-class backgrounds like mine. It was clear that solidarity was real, but so were the social fault lines, and, unsurprisingly, I felt much closer to the working-class participants from the Cape Flats. I attended several of these training programmes in the years to come. It was my first taste of how class and race could quietly undermine political unity.

After one of the subsequent ITP programmes, which usually took place in December, a friend from the Cape Flats, Abdur Razack, invited me to spend time with him and his family in Bonteheuwel, a working-class area with many of the social ills that come with being on the margins of society. Razack read widely, thought deeply about class and society, and was a deeply committed Muslim.

In my close to two months there, I had full days, including "stealing train" to get about because we hardly had money, political meetings and Muslim Students Association meetings at the University of the Western Cape campus, and all-night discussions on the latest political developments and what it meant to be an activist intellectual with oppression all around you. We certainly read a lot of Marx, but we also read Islamic Movement thinkers like Maududi and Shariati. In thinking about the re-ordering of society, we had to think about the possibilities of reconciling the insurgent religiosity of thinkers like Shariati with Marxism, if that was at all possible. Shariati's idea of the 'Muslim Marxist' was, not surprisingly, debated for hours.

We had some close calls with gangsters and those who were meant to enforce "the law", but these discussions in the midst of poverty, drug lords and gang wars piqued my intellectual appetite and made me think even more deeply about class and inequality. I still recall the amazing warmth and hospitality of Razack's parents, especially his mum. Despite being in a modest home in a poor, troubled neighbourhood, she treated us with generous meals, deep care, and the warmth and graciousness that's often typical of those with little means. This period left an indelible mark and helped shape my developing thinking and growing political consciousness.

By my late teens, I was angry at the inequality I saw, at the layers of prejudice — not just race and class — but also within the Indian Muslim community itself. In the broader context of that community, my family and similar families were largely invisible. One had to fight hard to ensure that one's views and existence were not dismissed. At school and on sports fields, there were subtle but unmistakable signals. I became aware that surnames defined you. Even within a community that was supposed to be united, there were hierarchies. I only came to understand the full weight of that history later.

When I completed matric, my results were good enough to get into university, but money was tight. My interest had always been politics — not only as activism, but also as something to study and understand in depth. Still, I doubted whether university was realistic for the simple reason that we had no money. People like us didn't go to university. I applied for and was offered a menial job at a local textile factory, where my father knew the owner.

I remember feeling excited at the prospect of making my own money as I sat in a barber's chair on the afternoon before I was due to start at the factory. But when I got home, my father said no. He told me to go and register at the university. He didn't know how we'd pay for it, but he said he could raise the registration fee and we'd "worry about the rest later". He was right — between a religious organisation and family friends, the money came together.

I registered at the University of Durban-Westville and was hopeful I'd find Muslim activists as politically progressive as those I'd met at the MYM's Islamic Training Programme. But while there was activism and thinking about Muslimness, it wasn't as radical or as well-theorised as I'd hoped. I found that kind of energy in the wider student community — among South African Students Congress members, left-wing student groups, and lecturers who had been in exile or the underground.

Figures like John Daniel, who had returned from exile, were inspiring. He taught political science with depth and urgency, connecting theory to the lived realities of liberation movements. A hugely decent man, Daniel would go on to play a large role in my adult life, becoming a really inspiring figure. David Hemson, whose radicalism I only came to fully appreciate later, was also a significant figure on campus. I didn't personally know Percy Mabogo More, but he was also a significant personality, as was Richard Pithouse, a charismatic young lecturer just a couple of years older than me. These people didn't just teach — they modelled an intellectual commitment to justice.

I was still at university and twenty years old when my dad collapsed at home one afternoon. I accompanied him to the hospital, seated near him in the ambulance. A close friend, Yunus, met me at the hospital to lend support and stood with me over the hard days that followed. When, after three tough days in the hospital, I returned home to take a quick break, the dreaded call came: "We'd like you to come to the hospital immediately." As an only child, this was particularly chilling.

I knew what lay in store. My father held my hand as I sat at his bedside. I think he was trying to advise an angry young man about navigating a harsh world. As his grip loosened and he slipped away, I knew that the real cause of his death was the rigours and exhaustion of life on the margins. A close friend, Yunus, was there and offered the support I needed. I had now become the breadwinner, caring for my mum. She passed away a few years later too.

In the weeks that followed, I had to ensure that I found a job, and I worked every weekend and hustled to make ends meet. Some family members helped. At the evening prayer, someone I knew from the Islamic Movement placed his hand around me and asked, "How will you pay the rent this month?" "I don't know," I said. With a reassuring smile on his face, he asked how much the rent was. "R 700," I replied. He placed his hand in his pocket and placed R 2 000 in my hand. "I think that will help," he said. That act, too, left an indelible mark. Kindness matters.

As things became harder, a professor who knew me at university often checked in. At first, I was too proud to say yes to the groceries he said he'd arrange, but after a while, I agreed. His caring gesture also stayed with me. When he called me to ask my view on a political issue recently, I reminded him of his kindness some thirty years ago. He only vaguely remembered. Or maybe he pretended not to remember because he saw it as an awkward moment.

After obtaining my four-year education degree, I graduated into a job market frozen by a government rationalisation plan that closed teacher training colleges and cut posts. I was supporting my mother and, needing to find work, I took a job teaching English at the private Orient Islamic School. I had my critiques of private Islamic education, but the principal was supportive, even allowing me to leave early twice a week so I could attend my master's lectures at the University of Natal's Institute for Social and Economic Research. A PhD in political sociology that straddled South Africa, and the Netherlands would follow some years later.

I met my wife in the aftermath of the World Conference on Racism. We moved to England when she was offered a post, as a medical doctor, in Sheffield. At first, I didn't have a job. I'd wander around Sheffield University during the day, hearing lecturers talk about Nelson Mandela and South African politics. An agency eventually placed me in a rough working-class high school in South Yorkshire. I was drawn to these kinds of towns, but they could be volatile. In my first week at a school in Doncaster, a pupil was stabbed. I'd thought South Africa was tough — but this was another level. I didn't last long there, moving on to teach in other schools across South Yorkshire. I got to know the rhythms and resilience of these communities, their humour too.

From England, I travelled to Ireland, where one day in Dublin, I had an unexpected encounter. I was on a bus when I spotted a familiar figure walking down the street. "I think that's Gerry Adams from the IRA," I said to my wife, Azeema Khan. She insisted it couldn't be — Adams was supposed to be in Belfast. But I got off at the next stop and walked up to him.

He greeted me warmly. When I told him I was from the University of Durban-Westville and knew he had visited there before, he invited me to the Sinn Féin offices nearby. The walls were covered in posters of Mandela, Yasser Arafat, and the Palestine Liberation Organisation. I didn't yet know the full history of the relationship between the IRA and the Palestinian struggle, but standing there, I could see it was a living connection — part of a shared international tradition of resistance. It was one of those moments when the world suddenly opens.

When we got back to South Africa, I got a call from Pithouse, who offered me a one-year post at UDW, teaching in the academic development programme. It was a risk — the university was chaotic and in crisis, and the job was less secure than teaching at a school — but I wanted to be in a space where I could combine teaching with political work. This decision connected me to a vibrant intellectual and political world that deeply shaped who I became.

Later on, I ran into John Daniel, who was now heading the South African programme of the School for International Training (SIT) in the building we shared with the Centre for Public Participation, where I was working with Janine Hicks. Daniel had a group of American students with him. I joked about what he was doing "with all these Americans", and he told me to give them a class — right there and then — on local government and public participation. They were wide-eyed, engaged, and full of questions. Daniel said, "You see? Don't write people off just because they're American. Some of them are here to learn and to contribute." It shifted my thinking.

He later fought for me to be appointed as the academic director of the SIT programme — even when the US office resisted because I didn't yet have a PhD. He argued that my lived experience in South Africa counted for more than formal credentials. When SIT finally offered me the job, they said I'd have to travel to Vermont for training. I hesitated. It was soon after 9/11, and with my skin colour and name, I was worried about how I'd be treated by US immigration. Daniel told me I was being paranoid, but I couldn't shake it.

The next day, I went to him and said, "John, I'll go — but only if you come with me." He asked, "Why should I go? They're paying for you, not me." I told him I really wanted him there, that I'd feel safer if he were with me. He pulled out his credit card, tossed it to me, and said, "I don't know how to book these things online — do it for me."

We landed in New York, and I was tense going through immigration. Daniel had been to the US dozens of times, but for me it was the first time. "Don't worry," he joked, "if they take you away, I'll tell your wife." The immigration officer — an African American woman — looked at my passport, smiled warmly and said, "Oh, you're from South Africa? I've been to Kruger National Park." I thought it was some kind of trick, but I told her I knew the park well. She stamped my passport and said, "Welcome to the United States."

There were many more trips to New York and Boston. On one of these trips, I noticed Daniel wasn't eating much except for some yoghurt. On his return to South Africa, he was diagnosed with cancer and passed away a few months later. Daniel was the consummate example of what we all strive for, but few ever attain. He had an unwavering commitment to justice and taught me lessons about questioning authority, reading widely, feeling deeply, and always demanding a better world. He was a provocateur, intellectual heavyweight and devoted educator.

Later, Kessie Moodley invited me to teach at the Workers' College, a trade union education project. There, I taught modules on globalisation and political theory to trade unionists — some with little formal education. It was a practical, democratic political education. The years I spent there were fundamental to my development and gave me a deep sense of what working-class life was like for others as I was moving into the middle class.

My first real taste of political work outside South Africa came through the Workers' College. In around 1999 Moodley invited me to join him on a trip to Matola, Mozambique, to run a workshop with the Mozambican trade union movement. It was also at this time that I connected with the Frelimo Party School and facilitated political education workshops for young Frelimo activists. There was a language barrier, but interpreters bridged the gap, and I always found the energy and commitment in the room electrifying.

It was also around this time that I met Ashraf Cassiem from the Anti-Eviction Campaign on a trip to Cape Town. Cassiem was an incredibly impressive activist, and the Anti-Eviction Campaign was the most radical of the new social movements that emerged at the time. This encounter began my interest in community-based organising.

I began travelling regularly: to Madagascar, Zambia, Namibia, Mozambique, and other countries in Southern Africa. In West Africa, it was to Senegal and Ghana, and in East Africa, it was to Kenya and Tanzania. In each place, I was struck by how particular political cultures shaped the work. In Zambia, workshops opened with religious songs and prayers, and there was a deep current of what people called "Christian socialism", drawing on the legacy of President Kenneth Kaunda. In

Madagascar, the poverty in Antananarivo and in the rural south was stark, but the activists I met there were resourceful and creative, even when working with almost nothing. In Namibia, the union movement was more structured and professionalised, but still deeply engaged in grassroots struggles.

These experiences taught me that political education isn't just about delivering content. It's about meeting people where they are — in their language, their traditions, their realities — and finding the points where solidarity can be built. Real political education is also a process of mutual learning, and I always learnt as much as I taught.

Back in Durban, I first learned about Abahlali baseMjondolo through conversations with Pithouse and Fazel Khan, a comrade from my student days. I was struck by how shack dwellers were organising themselves to defend their right to the city, resist eviction and speak in their own name. Coming from an ANC background, it wasn't easy to accept the depth of their critique of the party, but over time, it became clear that their warnings about neoliberalism, state violence and the steady gangsterisation of politics were not only justified — they were prescient.

Their members were fighting not for abstract policy promises, but for the immediate right to stay on the land they occupied, for decent housing, for safety from the police and party thugs. I respected their insistence on speaking for themselves, their refusal to be patronised by NGOs or political parties, and their sheer courage. In a world in which politics was becoming more grubby by the day, S'bu Zikode and others in the movement offered a principled alternative.

The spirit I'd first felt as a teenager stays with me — the combination of moral conviction and political clarity that I'd first glimpsed at the Islamic Training Programme.

Meetings with other political figures have shaped me, too. Having the chance to talk to the late Aziz Pahad, a former deputy foreign minister, over lunches and after his lectures on foreign policy to my students, was enlightening. So too were my engagements with Albie Sachs (one of South Africa's first Constitutional Court judges) in a similar context and the many exchanges of ideas with an intellectual heavyweight like South Africa's first post-apartheid transport minister, Mac Maharaj. Being at his 90th birthday and hearing him reminisce about his colourful past and clandestine escapades was very special.

I have been one of the lucky ones, one of a few who were able to move from a hard life, materially, into a middle-class life as apartheid came to an end. Millions of others have not been able to escape poverty. In some sense, the political climate is more crushing now that people no longer have a sense that there is an oppressive system that will inevitably give way to a more just society. Pessimism and cynicism are very common. Many people succumb to depression or damaging behaviours of various kinds rather than organising for a better life, a better society, a better world. This book comes out of my experience and my attempt to link what I have learned from the education I have had, from the people I have met, and from the reading I have been able to do, to the reality of South African life, and to think through it in a global context.

One part of the problem in South Africa has been the unfavourable global environment that emerged at the end of the Cold War — the dominance of the United States, the normalisation of neoliberalism, and the narrowing of perceived alternatives. But there have also been two equally decisive internal failures. The first has been a profound corruption of the vision of national liberation, with a class within that project actively making its compromises with capitalism and neoliberalism, and misrepresenting its own interests as those of the nation. The second has been the emergence of a deeply corrupt class, concerned chiefly with its own enrichment and power.

There have been important gains since 1994. The social grant system sustains millions of people. The ARV rollout keeps HIV-positive people alive. There has been expanded access to universities and significant investments in services and public institutions. But none of this has overcome the structural inequalities of our society, and much of it has been undermined by corruption, clientelism, and mismanagement. There are many senses in which things are getting worse as gangsterised forms of politics become increasingly powerful and mass systemic impoverishment and unemployment become ever more entrenched.

We must face the fact that the values of the national liberation movement are under sustained assault from corruption, gangsterised forms of politics, and complicity with neoliberalism. Yet the values of human rights are not exhausted. South Africa's decision to bring a case of genocide against Israel at the International Court of Justice, and the role it has played in initiating and guiding the Hague Group, are a testament to the endurance of those values in our public life.

In the face of enormous pressure from the United States and its allies, South Africa has asserted a moral and political leadership rooted in the anti-apartheid struggle's original commitments to justice, equality and solidarity. It has been shown that our country can still stand with the oppressed, speak truth to power, and help to build global alliances capable of confronting the most powerful states. That leadership is not a relic of the past, but a living possibility — one that can be renewed and deepened if it is anchored in a politics that serves the many rather than the few.

Corruption corrodes public trust, wastes resources, and erodes the very capacity of the state to meet people's needs. Honest officials work within a system where it is often impossible to get even the most basic work done without navigating demands for bribes or favours. Tenders are manipulated to benefit the connected rather than the competent. The looting of state resources for personal gain is not a marginal problem — it has become a defining feature of our political economy.

Violence is another defining feature of our crisis. We live in one of the most violent societies in the world, where murder, rape, and armed robbery are daily realities. Political violence has returned, too, often targeting grassroots activists. There is a grim familiarity to the stories: a leader receives threats, reports them to the police, and is then assassinated with little prospect that the killers will ever face justice. Violence is also embedded in the everyday experience of poor communities, from gang rule to domestic abuse, and it corrodes the possibility of democratic life.

Poverty and inequality remain stark. The end of formal apartheid did not dismantle the deep structures of racial capitalism. While poverty remains overwhelmingly Black, the elite and middle class have been significantly deracialised. At the same time, unemployment has reached staggering levels, especially among young people, leaving millions without hope of a better future.

Repression has been another constant. Protests are often met with police violence, including rubber bullets and live ammunition. Grassroots activists are harassed, arrested on trumped-up charges, or subjected to smear campaigns. The aim is often to break organisations before they can build sustained power.

Fascist politics are gaining ground, combining authoritarianism, militarism, and xenophobia. We have seen the rise of political actors who cultivate fear, identify scapegoats, and mobilise hatred to build their base. What has happened in India in recent years shows just how dangerous fascism can be, and how it can crush democratic hope and possibility in a society.

Internationalism remains essential. We cannot build a just South Africa in isolation from the world. Brutal sectarianism and a damaging desire for power have too often undermined progressive politics internationally. But solidarity, shared learning, and coordinated action remain vital.

Our problems are not unique. The same forces of neoliberalism, elite capture, and authoritarian politics are at work across the globe. However, there is no room for complacency or defeatism. Around the world, we have seen progressive political projects that have made a real difference by engaging ordinary people with respect and empathy, and helping to build their power.

This was achieved in our own history by the trade union movement following the Durban strikes in 1973 and by the United Democratic Front after its launch in Cape Town in 1983. It is seen today in the work of many social movements. But this needs to be achieved on a much bigger scale if we are to have any chance of resolving our fundamental problems.

Building mass democratic power that can confront both the state and capital is essential. But popular power also needs to be transformed into a viable electoral project. The South African left has failed to achieve this in 30 years, and we need to look at examples — such as in Latin America, including Bolivia, Brazil, and Colombia — where this has been achieved.

There is nowhere in the world where responses to injustice have resolved all problems. But there has been significant progress under progressive governments in a number of countries, despite severe national and international backlash. We need to study and learn from the best of these examples, to understand what can be done in building movements and political parties capable of real change. Our future depends on whether we can rebuild a politics that is rooted in the everyday lives and struggles of ordinary people, that treats them with respect, and that can turn their collective power into a transformative force.

CHAPTER 1

National Liberation Movements in Decline

A Moment of Transition

In May 2024, South Africa entered a new phase in its post-apartheid history. For the first time since 1994, the ANC was unable to secure a parliamentary majority. Thirty years after leading the country into democracy, the ANC was forced into a coalition arrangement, its dominance diminished and its moral authority threadbare. The party that had once been the primary political vehicle for the aspirations of the oppressed now found itself a shadow of its former self — fractured, directionless, and increasingly treated with scepticism by a younger generation for whom its heroic past no longer carried political weight.

But this is not simply a South African story. The long arc of the ANC's rise and decline echoes a broader continental pattern. Across Africa, national liberation movements that led anti-colonial struggles and held popular legitimacy at the moment of independence have, almost without exception, entered into periods of political decay. In many cases, they have collapsed entirely or survive only by abandoning democracy. This arc — from revolutionary idealism to state capture, from moral leadership to moral crisis — is not unique; it is typical.

Throughout the 1950s, '60s, and '70s, the African continent was ablaze with the fires of liberation. Movements led by figures like Kwame Nkrumah in Ghana, Amílcar Cabral in Guinea-Bissau, and Julius Nyerere in Tanzania were not only political movements; they were also deeply intellectual and philosophical projects. Their leaders wrote, theorised, and governed with a sense of historical responsibility. As Cabral put it: "We must act as if we answer to, and only answer to, our ancestors, our children, and the unborn."

But over time, many of these movements, once forged in struggle and idealism, calcified into authoritarian rule, corrupt patronage networks, and bureaucracies more interested in retaining power than transforming society. As Cabral warned, liberation must not become a new form of domination: "We are fighting so that insults may no longer rule our countries, martyred and scorned for centuries, so that our peoples may never more be exploited by imperialists — not only by people with white skin, because we do not confuse exploitation or exploiters with the colour of men's skins; we do not want any exploitation in our countries, not even by black people."

In Mozambique, Angola, and Zimbabwe, liberation movements remained in power by jettisoning democratic commitments and turning toward repression. In Ghana, Kenya, and Zambia, they were ousted through coups or lost power through the ballot.

South Africa's ANC, along with Namibia's Swapo, are among the last liberation movements on the continent still governing under a democratic framework. But the cracks have long been visible.

In South Africa, the seeds of this decay were sown early. As former ANC intelligence minister Ronnie Kasrils has written, reflecting on the legacy of the Freedom Charter: "In the 1980s, the [Freedom] Charter had been a call for deep structural transformation. At the settlement, key clauses — particularly those calling for the redistribution of land and the sharing of national wealth — were softened or deferred. The final settlement preserved existing patterns of private property and accepted a macroeconomic framework shaped in part by global neoliberal pressures. While the vote was won, the deeper transformations envisioned in the Charter were postponed. The result is that today, 31 years after the end of apartheid, structural inequalities and mass impoverishment remain."

Indeed, the ANC's embrace of neoliberal economic policy in the mid-1990s, its increasing entanglement with corporate elites, and the consolidation of patronage networks in local and provincial structures set the stage for a slow but persistent erosion of credibility. That this process happened gradually — interrupted by moments of rhetorical renewal or moral theatre — only masked the depth of the party's decline. As the chapters that follow will show, the consequences of this degeneration have been profound: the undermining of public institutions, the explosion of elite corruption, and the normalisation of political violence.

Frantz Fanon warned that national liberation movements could themselves become repressive: "The party, a true instrument of power in the hands of the bourgeoisie, reinforces the machine, and ensures that the people are hemmed in and immobilised. The party helps the government to hold the people down." When that warning is ignored, the distance between rulers and the ruled becomes insurmountable — and history, in its own time, moves on.

South Africa is not alone. From Accra to Dar es Salaam, Luanda to Maputo, the same pattern has repeated itself. A movement born in struggle loses its way in power. A movement that once drew strength from the people begins to fear them. A movement that promised liberation begins to protect privilege.

But decline is not inevitable. Renewal is possible.

The High Tide of Liberation

Between the mid-1950s and the 1970s, the African continent was swept by a powerful tide of liberation. In Namibia and South Africa, the struggle continued through the 1980s. For a time, it seemed as though the world was being remade. A generation of national liberation movements — grounded in mass organisation, animated by a democratic and internationalist spirit — rose to end centuries of colonial domination and racial subjugation.

These were movements forged in sacrifice, struggle, and deep popular commitment. Their leadership was often marked not only by strategic acumen and moral clarity but by intellectual seriousness. Leaders such as Nkrumah in Ghana, Nyerere in Tanzania, Cabral in Guinea-Bissau and Cape Verde, Samora Machel in Mozambique, and Patrice Lumumba in the Congo were not simply statesmen. They were theorists of liberation — figures who sought to think through, and act on, the great questions of their time: What would real freedom look like? How could societies rebuild on just foundations after centuries of exploitation? What kind of state, what kind of economy, what kind of citizen, should be built in the wake of empire?

This period was marked by an extraordinary sense of ambition. The goal was not just to replace colonial administrators with national elites. The task was much more expansive: to reimagine society from the ground up, rooted in justice, dignity, and sovereignty.

For Nyerere, the answer lay in Ujamaa, a form of African socialism premised on collective life and mutual responsibility. For Cabral, national liberation could only be meaningful if it resulted in "the liberation of the process of development of national productive forces." For Machel, the goal was not simply freedom for Mozambique, but solidarity with all who struggled. As he famously declared: "International solidarity is not an act of charity: it is an act of unity between allies fighting on different terrains toward the same objective."

These were not isolated efforts. From Ghana to India, from Tanzania to Cuba, movements and leaders shared ideas, tactics, and moral frameworks. Many were in conversation with one another — exchanging letters, hosting delegations, offering training, building alliances. There was a real sense of historical urgency: a conviction that a different world was not only necessary, but possible.

This was also a period in which South Africa's liberation struggle — though still confined under apartheid's boot — drew strength from continental and global shifts. The adoption of the Freedom Charter in 1955 placed South Africa squarely within this wider movement. The Charter's vision of shared wealth, democratic power, and racial equality resonated deeply with the aspirations being articulated elsewhere in the Global South.

The anti-apartheid movement received material and moral support from newly liberated African states. Tanzania and Zambia hosted exiled South African activists and allowed them to set up camps for military training. Algeria trained MK cadres. The global anti-colonial movement created a new moral consensus — one that delegitimised apartheid and gave strength to resistance within South Africa.

This high tide of liberation was not only about asserting sovereignty or removing colonial flags. It was about building egalitarian societies and forging a collective, post-imperial future. These were movements animated by a profound ethical commitment — to the wretched of the Earth, to the dignity of the oppressed, and to the unfinished task of decolonisation.

In 1957, Ghana became the first country in sub-Saharan Africa to win independence. Led by Nkrumah and the Convention People's Party, Ghana's liberation was an event of enormous symbolic significance. It marked the beginning of the end for European empires on the continent and lit a beacon for other struggles still to come.

Nkrumah was not only a political leader; he was a philosopher and a committed pan-Africanist. He believed that the liberation of any one African country would remain incomplete unless it was followed by the unification and emancipation of the entire continent. Pan-Africanism, for Nkrumah, was not only a cultural and political ideal — it was a strategy to break the grip of colonial division and build a common front against imperialism. He became a continental figure — admired by many, but feared by some at home — as he called for a United States of Africa and sought to fuse political sovereignty with economic justice. He grounded his ideas in the need to unify theory and practice, insisting that "practice without thought is blind; thought without practice is empty".

But while Nkrumah's early years in office were marked by ambitious development plans and deep international prestige, disillusionment set in quickly. As with so many national liberation movements, the immense challenges of governance under global capitalist constraints made ideals difficult to realise.

Economic difficulties mounted, and state-led development became associated with inefficiency and elite enrichment. Political opposition was increasingly suppressed, and democratic openings narrowed.

In 1966, Nkrumah was overthrown in a military coup while on a diplomatic mission abroad. The coup was backed by Western intelligence services, but it also reflected popular discontent. Ghana's economy was in decline, and resentment toward authoritarianism had begun to spread. What had begun as a revolutionary project ended in a growing perception of stagnation and betrayal.

The fall of Nkrumah's government marked the first major rupture in the dream of post-colonial transformation. It was a cautionary tale: that charismatic leadership and anti-colonial legitimacy were no guarantee of lasting justice or democracy. Ghana's trajectory was a sign that the forces arrayed against genuine liberation — both internal and external — were formidable, and that without deep democratic participation, even the most inspiring movements could falter.

Lessons from Tanzania and Zambia

In the aftermath of independence, few leaders on the continent carried as much moral authority as Tanzania's Nyerere and Zambia's Kaunda. Both men were central to the liberation of Southern Africa — not only as political figures within their own countries but as continental leaders who offered sanctuary, solidarity, and material support to liberation movements in Mozambique, Zimbabwe, Namibia, and South Africa. Their role in shaping the political character of the region cannot be overstated. And yet, while their integrity and internationalist commitments stood in contrast to the emerging kleptocracies in Angola or Zimbabwe, their experience also reveals the structural limits of postcolonial state-building — especially within the framework of the one-party state.

Nyerere, often referred to as Mwalimu (teacher), grounded his vision of Tanzanian socialism in the philosophy of Ujamaa — a model of collective development rooted in rural cooperation, self-reliance, and egalitarian values. He eschewed the trappings of personal wealth and power and was admired across Africa and beyond for his austere and principled leadership.

However, Ujamaa's implementation proved far more difficult than its ideals. The forced relocation of peasants into collective villages often produced dislocation rather than empowerment. Agricultural production declined, and many communities resisted what they experienced as top-down social engineering. Moreover, the concentration of political power in the ruling Chama Cha Mapinduzi party, which Nyerere led, left little space for political dissent or independent organising. The ban on opposition parties, rationalised as a bulwark against ethnic division and instability, ultimately stifled democratic development.

Still, Nyerere's integrity remained widely respected. He voluntarily stepped down from power in 1985 — a rare act in post-independence Africa — and continued to play a critical role in regional diplomacy, most notably in the effort to end apartheid. As he put it, "Leadership is not a matter of talking, it is a matter of doing". His tenure illustrated the tension between revolutionary ideals and institutional constraints, between moral authority and the reality of governing under conditions of deep structural inequality and economic dependency.

Zambia under Kaunda offers a parallel, though distinct, trajectory. Kaunda's United National Independence Party came to power in 1964 with a message of national unity and African humanism. Like Nyerere, Kaunda styled himself as a moral leader rather than a populist strongman. He too aligned himself with liberation struggles across the region and positioned Zambia as a frontline state in the fight against apartheid and white minority rule. Lusaka hosted the exiled leadership of the ANC and Swapo, and bore the brunt of retaliatory raids from Rhodesian and South African forces.

Domestically, however, Kaunda's long rule — stretching across four terms — slowly hardened into authoritarianism. In 1972, Zambia became a one-party state, a move that Kaunda defended as necessary to prevent ethnic and regional fragmentation. As with Nyerere, the logic of stability was used to narrow the political space. Corruption and economic mismanagement — amplified by the collapse of global copper prices — deepened public disillusionment. By the late 1980s, Zambia faced widespread unrest, and Kaunda, to his credit, responded not with force but with political reform. He allowed for multi-party elections in 1991 and accepted electoral defeat with grace, setting a precedent for peaceful democratic transition that remains exceptional on the continent.

Together, the Tanzanian and Zambian experiences illuminate the complex legacy of post-independence leadership. On one hand, these leaders were principled internationalists who gave material and diplomatic support to freedom movements across Southern Africa. They governed with relative restraint, upheld norms of personal probity, and maintained a language of justice and solidarity that resonated across the continent. On the other hand, their embrace of the one-party state, their suppression of opposition, and the failure of state-led economic models raise difficult questions about the relationship between ideals and institutions.

Their stories also challenge the idea that the decline of liberation movements is inevitable. Unlike other contexts where power was used to accumulate private wealth or entrench political dynasties, both Nyerere and Kaunda accepted limits on personal wealth, on terms in office, and ultimately on their hold on power. They exited not in disgrace but in humility. Yet their departures left fragile institutions behind. The transition to multi-party democracy in both countries was bumpy, and economic liberalisation under structural adjustment programmes hollowed out much of the public good they had sought to build.

In reflecting on these experiences, it becomes clear that post-liberation governance is a long and often painful negotiation between revolutionary ambition and the realities of constrained sovereignty, economic dependency, and political compromise. The example of Tanzania and Zambia shows that personal integrity, while essential, is not sufficient to sustain democratic transformation. Without institutions capable of embedding accountability, participation, and public ownership over development, the vision of liberation can fade — even in the hands of its most committed stewards.

India: The Long Arc of Postcolonial Decay

India's postcolonial trajectory offers another instructive case of a liberation movement that began with idealism and ended in betrayal. The Indian National Congress (INC), which led the anti-colonial struggle against British rule, was once widely admired as a party of ethical leadership, pluralism, and social reform.

Under Jawaharlal Nehru, India's first prime minister, the Congress Party stood for secularism, non-alignment in the Cold War, and a commitment to planning and redistribution within a democratic framework. Nehru spoke of building a society rooted in "scientific temper", egalitarianism, and peaceful coexistence. In its early decades, India held regular elections, protected free speech, and built up a state committed, at least in principle, to addressing poverty, caste inequality, and the legacies of colonial economic underdevelopment.

But this vision began to falter within a generation. From the 1970s onward, India entered a period of creeping authoritarianism, elite consolidation, and widening inequality. The 1975–77 Emergency, during which Indira Gandhi suspended constitutional rights, imposed censorship, and jailed political opponents, marked a sharp departure from the founding ideals of the republic. While India remained formally democratic, political power became increasingly dynastic, and the Congress Party became more centralised and disconnected from its popular base.

The shift to neoliberal economic policy in the 1990s, carried out by the Congress itself, accelerated the erosion of the party's moral legitimacy. Deregulation, privatisation, and the opening of markets to foreign capital were promoted as necessary modernisation. But they also deepened inequality, disempowered the poor, and widened the distance between India's governing elites and its rural and working class majority.

Structural adjustment measures imposed by global financial institutions led to the abandonment of food subsidies, cutbacks in education and healthcare, and the dispossession of marginalised communities. The INC, once the political vehicle of independence, had become the manager of a neoliberal order deeply hostile to the very people whose hopes it once carried.

The transition from the Congress Party's pluralist and inclusive secular nationalism to the authoritarian Hindu nationalism of the Bharatiya Janata Party (BJP) is not just a story of political competition. It reflects a deeper process in which the promise of national liberation was slowly hollowed out, leaving space for a new elite to remake the nation in their image.

The rise of Hindutva — a chauvinistic, authoritarian project grounded in Hindu majoritarianism — represents not merely a political shift, but the ascendance of a deeply exclusionary nationalism that seeks to erase the pluralistic foundations of modern India. Propounded by the Rashtriya Swayamsevak Sangh — a right-wing volunteer paramilitary organisation — and given political expression through the BJP, Hindutva aims to transform India into a Hindu-first state.

This project has involved ideological revisionism, violent attacks on Muslims and Christians, and the suppression of dissent across civil society, media, and the academy. Its success cannot be separated from the failure of the Indian National Congress, which, through its embrace of neoliberalism, created the social despair and political vacuum in which fascism could flourish.

As Arundhati Roy has written, "Our tragedy is that once again we've been colonised, this time by our own elites." This betrayal of the postcolonial promise has made possible a new form of internal colonisation — one marked not by foreign conquest, but by the authoritarian rule of a communal elite.

Today, under the BJP, India faces the systematic dismantling of democratic institutions, from the judiciary to the press. The violence of the Hindu right is not incidental, but constitutive: lynchings, pogroms, and the incarceration of dissidents are central to the new order. In this light, Hindutva is not only a betrayal of India's founding vision, but a textbook example of how a national liberation movement, in failing to renew its commitments, can open the door to something far darker.

The Indian case also underscores the danger of elite nationalism — of a politics that mobilises the language of freedom, but in practice substitutes one ruling class for another. Despite universal suffrage and formal democracy, millions remain structurally excluded from land, education, and security. Dalits, Adivasis, Muslims, and the rural poor continue to bear the brunt of the violence, both economic and political, of a system that speaks the language of development while delivering dispossession.

The INC's decline, and the BJP's authoritarian rise, cannot be fully explained without acknowledging this slow-burning betrayal. Without structural transformation and real popular participation liberation curdles into resentment. And that resentment, if not organised into through democratic and egalitarian projects, becomes fertile ground for reactionary forces.

India's experience is a cautionary tale. It shows that without institutions rooted in popular control and genuine accountability, postcolonial democracies are vulnerable to capture — first by technocratic elites, then by demagogues. It also shows that elections alone are no safeguard against decay. When the substance of democracy is hollowed out, its form can be weaponised to legitimise tyranny.

In India today, the betrayal of the ideals that animated the anti-colonial movement is no longer a matter of elite drift — it has become an explicit programme. And yet, resistance continues: from farmers' movements to student uprisings, from feminist collectives to legal challenges in defence of civil liberties. The task remains what it has always been: to turn formal democracy into substantive freedom, and to complete the unfinished work of liberation.

Southern Africa: Revolution Delayed

In much of Africa, formal independence came during the 1950s and '60s. But in Southern Africa, liberation was delayed — and often more bitterly contested. Only in 1975 did Mozambique and Angola break free from Portuguese colonialism after a prolonged armed struggle. Zimbabwe followed in 1980, Namibia in 1990, and South Africa in 1994. These were hard-won victories, paid for in blood and achieved after decades of sacrifice, imprisonment, exile, and war.

Unlike many movements elsewhere on the continent that were later overthrown, Southern Africa's liberation parties have largely retained state power. Frelimo in Mozambique, the MPLA in Angola, Zanu-PF in Zimbabwe,

Swapo in Namibia, and the ANC in South Africa all continue to govern. Yet over time, the moral and political authority once granted by their historic role in defeating colonialism has eroded — the so-called liberation dividend has steadily declined.

Where these movements once promised egalitarian transformation, many have come to embody forms of authoritarianism and elite consolidation. In Angola, Mozambique, and Zimbabwe, ruling parties have presided over regimes of kleptocratic extraction, personal enrichment, and political violence. Zanu-PF, for instance, took over a land reform movement in the late 1990s not to genuinely redistribute land, but to legitimise itself while enriching its elites. A small coterie around the party leadership received vast tracts of land, while rural poverty and political repression intensified.

Namibia and South Africa followed a different trajectory, shaped more by protracted negotiations rather than, as the liberation movements in both countries had hoped, the armed seizure of power. But the result has not been dramatically different. Despite democratic constitutions, both countries have seen growing political exclusion, economic inequality, and the hollowing out of public institutions. In South Africa, this has included the turn to repression — most notoriously at Marikana in 2012, where 34 striking Lonmin platinum miners were killed by the police.

As Kasrils observed, reflecting on the compromises made during South Africa's transition: "In the 1980s, the [Freedom] Charter had been a call for deep structural transformation. At the settlement, key clauses — particularly those calling for the redistribution of land and the sharing of national wealth — were softened or deferred.

The final settlement preserved existing patterns of private property and accepted a macroeconomic framework shaped in part by global neoliberal pressures. While the vote was won, the deeper transformations envisioned in the Charter were postponed." The result, Kasrils concludes, is that decades after apartheid ended, "structural inequalities and mass impoverishment remain. The Charter's economic promises have not been fulfilled."

As the philosopher Michael Neocosmos has argued, the transition to democracy in South Africa entailed not only a political compromise, but a deeper substitution of one mode of politics for another. During the 1980s, the struggles that animated township life and rural resistance were driven by what he calls people's politics — a political culture rooted in collective action, egalitarianism, and popular forms of decision-making.

These were often deeply democratic in form, with practices of consensus-building and grassroots deliberation. But as the ANC moved closer to formal negotiations, these popular energies were marginalised in favour of state politics — the politics of parties, elites, and technocratic management. In this shift, the emancipatory thrust of the liberation movement was disciplined into a logic of state power, increasingly reliant on bureaucratic authority and coercion rather than popular legitimacy.

Neocosmos warns that this narrowing of political space resulted in a profound "closure of the political", in which ordinary people were told that politics now belonged to experts, parliamentarians, and party functionaries. The effects of this closure remain with us: protest is routinely criminalised, dissent is met with repression, and autonomous political subjectivities are treated not as legitimate democratic actors, but as threats to order.

In this sense, the degeneration of the liberation project in South Africa was not simply a betrayal of its economic promises, but a foreclosure of its democratic possibilities. The very people who brought the country to the brink of change were pushed back into the margins once state power was secured.

As in other parts of the continent, the degeneration of the liberation tradition in Southern Africa has been uneven but undeniable. Political repression, elite capture, and moral exhaustion are now hallmarks of governments that once stood for freedom and dignity. Their continued dominance owes less to popular mobilisation than to control over state resources, entrenched party machinery, and, in some cases, open violence. The promises of liberation remain unfulfilled, even as the language of struggle is repurposed to justify a new form of rule.

The decline of the ANC reached its nadir in the Jacob Zuma era. Under Zuma's leadership, the ANC was engulfed in state-capture scandals that devastated public institutions and eroded trust. Corruption became endemic, service delivery faltered, factional battles destabilised governance, and repression escalated sharply.

Today, the ANC faces an unprecedented crisis. Yet the legacy of the ANC's liberation struggle still casts a long shadow. Its history is woven into the fabric of the nation, and its moral authority, though diminished, continues to shape political discourse. The challenge now is whether the party can undergo the profound renewal required to reclaim its founding ideals — or whether its decline will open the door to a fragmented and unstable political landscape.

South Africa's crisis is thus both unique and emblematic. It reflects the broader pattern experienced by national liberation movements across Africa and beyond: a trajectory from hopeful transformation to entrenched corruption and crisis. The question remains what comes next, and whether the ideals of freedom and equality can be rekindled from below.

CHAPTER 2

The Corruption Crisis

At the end of apartheid, the moral authority of the liberation struggle gave the new state a powerful foundation of popular legitimacy. That authority has been steadily corroded by a deep and pervasive crisis of corruption.

Today, the rot runs through almost every level of the state — from municipalities to national government. State institutions have been hollowed out. Procurement has become a site of looting. Budgets meant for clinics and classrooms, water pipes and housing, have been siphoned off through tenders designed to enrich connected elites.

The looting of public funds has often been brazen. People who became massively wealthy have often been celebrated, with some, like Durban 'tenderpreneur' Shauwn Mkhize, becoming celebrities. The rapid enrichment of politically connected people from public budgets has sometimes been heralded as if it were a fruit of the liberation struggle. At the heart of this crisis lies not only greed, but a systematic erosion of the idea of public service.

Many countries followed a similar trajectory after independence from colonialism, and we should have been prepared for the risks that corruption could become an overwhelming structural crisis. After all, while in exile many of the leaders in the ANC had witnessed how corruption had corroded social hopes in other African countries. Fanon, the great revolutionary philosopher, had written a scathing critique of postcolonial elites back in 1961. Novelists like Ayi Kwei Armah and Salman Rushdie had issued similar warnings.

Corruption is a global and often structural problem deeply connected to the global crisis of attacks on democracy and the rise of neoliberalism. In countries like Brazil, India, and the United States, we see similar patterns — state capture by elites, the monetisation of political access, and the subordination of the public good to private gain.

Yet what is particularly shocking and painful about the crisis of corruption in South Africa is the depth of the betrayal. A struggle waged in the name of justice and equality has given rise to a political order that reproduces the very inequalities it sought to undo and often protects them with violence.

The democratic institutions established after 1994 have not been dismantled, but they have been politicised, weakened, and often penetrated or even captured by criminal networks. As the Zondo Commission into state capture revealed in painstaking detail, this process of degradation was not incidental. It was planned, coordinated, and executed at the highest levels.

The growing convergence between political corruption and violent crime is particularly alarming. In parts of the country, with the province of KwaZulu-Natal being the most notorious, the political system has become entangled with networks involved in construction mafias, political assassinations, and protection rackets. The state is no longer simply corrupt — it is, in places, criminal.

The result is a legitimacy crisis that poses a direct threat to the future of democracy. When citizens see politicians enriching themselves while services collapse, they lose faith not only in political parties but in the idea of democratic politics itself. That vacuum is dangerous. It creates space for authoritarianism, for demagogues who promise to clean up corruption while entrenching their own networks of patronage.

It also deepens cynicism, disillusionment, and despair — especially among the youth. The fact that the majority of South Africans no longer bother to vote is a shocking indictment of the conduct of the political class over the last three decades. Out of a registered voter population of 27.7 million people, only 16.2 million cast their ballots in the 2024 elections.

But across the country, honest public servants continue to do their jobs under difficult conditions. Civil society organisations, investigative journalists, whistleblowers, and, above all, courageous grassroots activists, have stood firm in the face of intimidation and violence. Some judges and prosecutors have refused to bow to political pressure. The resilience of these people is a reminder that the democratic project is not yet defeated. They deserve our utmost respect and support.

The Origins of Systemic Corruption

The transition to democracy brought immense hope, but also structural vulnerabilities. The underground nature of the struggle meant that the ruling party emerged from the liberation struggle without a strong culture of institutional accountability. Power was concentrated in the hands of political leaders who were, understandably, lionised by the public. But this reverence soon created a culture of impunity. The failure to hold leaders accountable during the arms deal scandal in the late 1990s set a dangerous precedent. It signalled that those at the top could bend rules with few consequences.

Over time, this permissiveness calcified. Patronage networks developed within the ANC, blurring the lines between party and state. Cadre deployment — while originally promoted as a mechanism to transform the apartheid bureaucracy — soon became a system of rewarding political loyalty over competence. This weakened professional oversight and created fertile ground for corruption to thrive.

But the rise of corruption is not simply the story of immoral individuals exploiting a political culture of nepotism dressed up as transformation. To fully grasp the roots of systemic corruption in South Africa, it is essential to understand the broader shift in governance that occurred during the democratic transition and its aftermath. The story of corruption is also the story of how neoliberalism restructured the state, hollowed out public capacity, and created conditions in which private accumulation came to dominate public life.

The neoliberal turn began in earnest with the adoption of the Growth, Employment and Redistribution (Gear) strategy in 1996. This policy marked a sharp departure from the more redistributive instincts of the Reconstruction and Development Programme (RDP), which had promised significant investment in public infrastructure, land reform, and social welfare.

Under Gear, the state reoriented itself around fiscal discipline, trade liberalisation, and the outsourcing of public functions to the private sector. Austerity replaced redistribution. The public good was subordinated to market logics. The role of the state shifted from provider to regulator.

This shift had far-reaching consequences. Most significantly, it meant that the government no longer saw itself as the primary agent of development. Instead, it outsourced large portions of its responsibilities — housing, sanitation, infrastructure, even education and health services — to private companies, often through a tender system.

In theory, tenders were meant to ensure transparency and competition. In practice, they became a site of political contestation and a source of extraordinary rents. The tender system disarticulated service provision from accountability. It became a mechanism for accumulation, rather than a vehicle for public service delivery.

The Black Economic Empowerment (BEE) policy, introduced as a measure to redress apartheid-era exclusion, was grafted onto this new model in a way that further entrenched patronage. Instead of building a broad, transformative economic base, BEE often facilitated elite enrichment.

The state's procurement policies, now central to redistribution, created incentives for politically connected individuals to secure tenders and contracts. This did not mean that the transformation itself was the problem. On the contrary, genuine economic justice remains an urgent imperative. But the form that BEE took, within the neoliberal framework, politicised procurement and created new avenues for corruption.

As the South African writer and public intellectual William Gumede has noted, BEE was swiftly captured by a political elite. Instead of building capacity within the state to deliver services, the ANC outsourced state functions while simultaneously ensuring that those awarded tenders were often politically aligned. This fusion of market and political power undermined institutional integrity. It weakened the state's ability to perform even its most basic functions. And it created a system in which corruption was not an aberration but a structural feature.

'Tenderpreneurship' emerged not as an isolated phenomenon but as the dominant logic of political advancement. Political office became a mechanism for personal enrichment. Public procurement became less about public benefit and more about private accumulation.

The result is a political culture where corruption is not an anomaly but a mode of both governance and class formation.

State Capture

When Zuma ascended to the presidency in 2009, 'tenderpreneurship' was accelerated and deepened to unprecedented levels and provided the basis for much more far-reaching forms of looting public funds and institutions.

The story of state capture is now well known. A powerful network centred on the immigrant Gupta family was able to exercise immense influence over key state institutions, including Eskom, Transnet, and the South African Revenue Service (Sars). The scale of the looting was staggering. But what is equally important to understand is the political context that enabled it.

Zuma's rise was not inevitable. It was driven by a cynical alliance of opportunists within the ANC, such as Julius Malema, who headed the Youth League at the time. There was also a staggering failure of ethical and political judgment on the part of the left in the Congress alliance, most notably Blade Nzimande and the South African Communist Party (SACP), Zwelinzima Vavi and the leadership of the Congress of South African Trade Unions (Cosatu), who supported Zuma's rise to power, and even supported him during his rape trial. They championed

Zuma as a man of the people — an antidote to the perceived elitism of former president Thabo Mbeki. In doing so, they wilfully turned a blind eye to Zuma's corruption and authoritarianism, and to his deeply troubling record on gender.

Feminists warned against his rise. So did Abahlali baseMjondolo, which courageously opposed Zuma and his toxic ethnic nationalism from the start.

The support from the SACP and Cosatu for Zuma — often framed in the language of left populism — was particularly damaging. It gave his presidency a veneer of progressive legitimacy that masked the reality of the rise of a vicious counter-elite to both the old white elites and Mbeki's professionalised political and civil servant class. Once in power, Zuma hollowed out state institutions, appointed loyalists to key positions, and turned governance into a mechanism for rent extraction.

State capture was not only about the enrichment of the Guptas or Zuma himself. It was a systemic mode of rule in which institutions were repurposed to serve private and factional interests. Public appointments became instruments of loyalty. Oversight bodies were undermined or neutralised. Key state-owned enterprises were looted with impunity.

There was also an all-out attack on the integrity of the public sphere, some of it driven by the notorious British public relations firm Bell Pottinger working with local proxies, such as Andile Mngxitama and his made-for-television rent-a-crowd fake movement, Black First Land First.

The analysis of Ivor Chipkin and Mark Swilling has been especially important in understanding the systemic nature of state capture. They argue that South Africa experienced not only corruption at the level of individuals, but a rupture in the political-administrative interface of the state. The professional civil service was eroded, replaced by networks of patronage that bypassed institutional checks and balances.

This was not simply the result of moral and strategic failure but was a mode of governance that deliberately sought to reconfigure the state for private accumulation. They describe this as a shift from a bureaucratic state to a rent-seeking one, where political authority was used not to direct policy or development but to channel resources to connected elites. As Chipkin put it, "What we saw was not just theft, but a hostile takeover of the state".

The consequences were devastating. Billions of rand were lost. Infrastructure deteriorated. Public trust collapsed. The state's ability to provide even basic services was severely compromised.

The journalists and NGOs that opposed state capture often acted with courage, and the Gupta leaks were a seminal moment in the opposition to Zuma's kleptocracy. But this white-dominated middle-class opposition to Zuma via donor-funded NGOs and media was not without its own problems. Its sneering tone was often offensive to many Black South Africans, and the political project that emerged around it was dominated by middle-class and often white voices, backed by

Western donors and white businesses. It lacked the tone or political grounding to resonate widely across society.

There was no interest in building alliances with poor and working-class communities, and grassroots organisations and trade unions stayed well clear of organisations like Save South Africa. The high price that Abahlali baseMjondolo paid for their opposition to Zuma was largely ignored in the white-dominated middle-class NGO and media circles that saw themselves as the custodians of the struggle against Zuma.

For many within the ANC and its support base, the pushback against Zuma appeared less as a democratic renewal than a form of externally-driven regime change — a 'colour revolution'.

The failure to build a broad, popular and democratic opposition to Zuma was a missed opportunity, and it laid the foundation for the failure to root out corruption after he was hounded from office.

The dead-end of Ramaphoria

When President Cyril Ramaphosa took office in February 2018, following Zuma's resignation under immense internal and public pressure, a wave of cautious optimism swept through South Africa. The mood was dubbed "Ramaphoria" — a sense that, finally, the long night of state capture was over, and that a new era of ethical governance, competent administration, and constitutional renewal was at hand.

For a country exhausted by more than a decade of corruption and the decline of public services and institutions, Ramaphosa's ascension seemed to promise a return to moral and technocratic order. He positioned himself as a reformer, a pragmatist with strong struggle credentials and global credibility. His rhetoric was measured, his tone reassuring. And his early moves — appointing new boards to damaged institutions like Eskom and the revenue service, and committing to reform — won praise from local and international observers alike.

At the centre of this early reform agenda stood the Zondo Commission, formally launched in August 2018. Chaired by then Deputy Chief Justice Raymond Zondo, the commission was tasked with investigating the full extent of corruption and patronage networks that had flourished during the Zuma years.

Over nearly four years, the commission heard testimony from more than 300 witnesses, amassed vast volumes of documentation, and produced a five-part report running to thousands of pages. It was, by any standard, a monumental undertaking in the history of democratic accountability. For many, it became a national spectacle: a rolling drama in which the full horror of elite criminality was laid bare.

Some of the commission's most explosive findings included:

- Direct Gupta involvement in Cabinet appointments: Former deputy finance minister Mcebisi Jonas testified that the Gupta family offered him a R600 million bribe and promised him the finance ministry — months before the actual reshuffle. Jonas revealed that the Guptas claimed to control everything, including key decisions in government.

- Massive corruption at Eskom and Transnet: The commission found that Eskom had been reduced to a "feeding trough" for the Gupta network. Former executives Brian Molefe and Matshela Koko were implicated in engineering procurement deals for Gupta-linked firms such as Tegeta. At Transnet, similar patterns emerged — manipulated locomotive contracts, inflated pricing, and R41 billion in dubious transactions.
- The hollowing out of Sars: Under Tom Moyane, the South African Revenue Service was systematically dismantled. Its investigative capacity was weakened, its credibility destroyed. Zondo found this was not incompetence but part of a deliberate strategy to disable oversight institutions.
- The Bosasa bribery empire: Testimony from whistleblower Angelo Agrizzi revealed how Bosasa, a facilities management company, paid bribes to ministers, MPs, and civil servants in cash, luxury items, and monthly "retainers". The scale and banality of the corruption stunned even seasoned observers.
- ANC complicity: One of the most damning conclusions of the commission was its

indictment of the ANC itself. The party, it found, had failed to act on repeated warnings and evidence of corruption. Cadre deployment, it said, undermined meritocracy and enabled the entrenchment of patronage.

- Ramaphosa's own awareness: Crucially, the commission noted that Ramaphosa, while deputy president, was aware of much of what was unfolding. Though he may have been constrained by internal politics, his failure to act more decisively was seen by some as a form of complicity.

Despite the scale of the Zondo Commission's work and the clarity of its findings, the follow-through has been painfully slow. Few high-profile prosecutions have materialised. Key figures named in the report remain free. There has been no genuine political will to clean house.

Ramaphosa's presidency has increasingly come to be seen as defined more by inaction than bold reform. His approach — cautious, consultative, and always mindful of internal ANC dynamics —has failed to match the urgency of the moment.

More troubling still is the realisation that many of the networks that facilitated state capture remain intact. While the Guptas have fled the country, and Zuma no longer holds office, the deeper structural drivers of corruption — tender-based governance, cadre deployment, and party-state conflation — have not been dismantled. In fact, state capture has continued, and in some cases worsened, in a more decentralised, rhizomatic form.

The Zondo Commission remains a historic achievement. It has preserved memory, affirmed truth, and documented the betrayal of a people's trust in staggering detail. But commissions do not deliver justice. They provide evidence. And without political courage and mass mobilisation, evidence alone cannot dislodge entrenched power.

South Africans were right to hope for renewal in 2018. But as the years have passed, and Ramaphoria has faded into disillusionment, it has become clear that the path to democratic integrity requires more than courts and commissions. It demands a political rupture with elite impunity — and the reconstruction of public life from below.

Today, across the country, municipalities are paralysed by procurement delays, inflated costs, and chronic non-delivery. Provincial governments are often captured by patronage networks, their administrations hollowed out by cadre deployment. National departments, stripped of internal expertise and institutional memory, outsource core functions to consultants who charge exorbitant fees for often substandard work. A generation of capable public servants has been replaced, not by democratic participation or community oversight, but by politically connected middlemen profiting from the fragmentation of public authority.

This is not merely a story of poor management or individual failure. It reflects, as Pithouse has argued, a deeper problem: the corruption of the very idea of the public. Fighting corruption cannot be reduced to purging a few bad actors or improving compliance systems. It requires confronting the structural logic that has normalised private accumulation through public institutions.

A serious response to corruption must begin with a reckoning with the legacy of neoliberalism. This means rebuilding the state's capacity to deliver essential services directly. It means ending the overreliance on consultants and tenders, and reinvesting in the skills and integrity of a professional civil service. It means rejecting the idea that efficiency lies in market-based mechanisms, and instead reasserting the principle that public money must serve public needs.

None of this will be easy. A generation of political elites has come of age within the current system, often benefiting from it directly. Many will resist efforts to re-establish direct, accountable, and ethical public provision. But without such a shift, corruption will remain entrenched — not as an aberration, but as a symptom of a deeper dysfunction.

Reclaiming the state is not simply about better governance; it is a political and moral imperative. It is about restoring a sense of collective ownership over public institutions. It is about ensuring that the state serves the people, not the politically connected. And it is about rebuilding the infrastructure of a democratic society in which dignity, equity, and justice are not slogans, but lived realities.

This requires a strong critique of capital as well as the rotten parts of the political class. For all the public anger rightly directed at state corruption, it is striking how little attention has been paid to corporate malfeasance of comparable or even greater scale. The Steinhoff scandal, which erupted in late 2017, remains one of the largest instances of white-collar fraud in South African history —yet it never triggered the kind of public outrage or institutional scrutiny that accompanied the state-capture project.

At its height, Steinhoff International was a global retail giant, boasting an empire that stretched from Europe to Africa, with brands including Pep, Ackermans, Mattress Firm, and Conforama. Its CEO, Markus Jooste, was a poster boy for Afrikaner business success. But the company's spectacular collapse revealed a sprawling web of fictitious transactions, inflated profits, and hidden liabilities. The losses were staggering — more than R200 billion in shareholder value was wiped out almost overnight. Pension funds, including those of ordinary South African workers, were decimated. Yet Jooste remained a free man for years, protected by elite networks and the systemic inertia of South Africa's regulatory architecture.

The contrast with the Zondo Commission is revealing. While the commission spent years investigating and publicising the mechanics of state capture — culminating in volumes of testimony and recommendations — there has been no equivalent inquiry into Steinhoff. There has been no sustained national conversation about elite impunity in the private sector.

The media coverage, though critical at times, lacked the moral intensity and sustained campaigning that characterised the coverage of Zuma and the Guptas. And while whistleblowers in the public sector were often lauded (though not always protected), those who raised concerns in corporate environments were routinely sidelined or ignored.

This disparity is not accidental. It reflects a deeper ideological fault line in South African society: a tendency to locate corruption in the Black political class, while assuming that white capital is naturally efficient, rule-abiding, and ethical. The figure of the corrupt politician is typically imagined as a Black man in a designer suit, not a white man in a tailored blazer operating out of Stellenbosch. This racialised and classed construction of corruption distorts the national conversation and allows massive corporate fraud to fly under the radar of public accountability.

Moreover, elite corporate corruption is often transnational. In the case of Steinhoff, European banks, auditors, and regulators were implicated. This highlights the role of global capital and international finance in enabling and shielding corrupt practices. Unlike petty graft or even localised state capture, corporate corruption operates through complex financial instruments, tax havens, and legal loopholes — making it harder to detect and even harder to prosecute.

Steinhoff is not an outlier. The construction cartel, exposed during the infrastructure build-up to the 2010 FIFA World Cup, revealed how some of the country's most established firms colluded to inflate prices and defraud the state. Other sectors — such as healthcare, banking, and retail — have also seen price-fixing scandals and anti-competitive practices, with companies paying fines that amounted to little more than the cost of doing business. In 2007, major South African bread producers were found guilty of colluding to fix bread prices, driving up costs for millions of poor households. The Competition Commission fined companies like Pioneer Foods and Tiger Brands, exposing how corporate greed directly harmed the poor.

A credible anti-corruption agenda cannot afford to turn a blind eye to the private sector. To do so is to endorse a double standard — one in which Black political corruption is demonised, while white business corruption is sanitised, depoliticised, or ignored. True accountability requires parity of scrutiny. It requires confronting the complicity of elite networks, financial institutions, and corporate lawyers in systemic fraud. It requires new institutions, investigative capacity, and legal tools geared toward uncovering and prosecuting high-level economic crime in the private sector.

Corruption is not only a matter of brown envelopes handed over in dark corners or high-profile scandals like Steinhoff and state capture. It is also institutionalised through more subtle and structural mechanisms — one of the most important being the so-called revolving door between the state and the private sector.

In post-apartheid South Africa, the relationship between business and the state has grown increasingly porous. Senior public officials, cabinet ministers, and regulators frequently exit public office only to reappear months later as consultants, board members, or executives in the very industries they once oversaw. This creates powerful incentives to govern with one eye on the public interest and the other on future private enrichment. The effect is to erode public trust, compromise policy integrity, and entrench the influence of corporate interests within the machinery of the state.

The most notorious example is Eskom, where senior executives have frequently moved in and out of the private energy sector. This creates an environment in which long-term energy planning is subordinated to short-term profiteering. A similar pattern has played out in the telecommunications, health, and mining sectors — where former ministers or directors-general re-emerge in advisory roles, lobbying their former colleagues or drafting legislation that benefits their new employers. This is not simply lobbying. It is a capture of the policymaking process from the inside out.

The problem with the revolving door is not just one of perception. It institutionalises a form of corruption in which public actors do not act out of direct bribery or coercion but are structurally predisposed to act in ways that favour powerful private actors over the public good.

This is legal, but corrosive. And it helps to explain why so many policies — from energy procurement to pharmaceuticals — consistently favour elite interests despite strong evidence of their harm to broader society.

This problem has been supercharged by the neoliberal turn in the state. As public sector capacity has declined — due to austerity, outsourcing, and the valorisation of private-sector "efficiency" — the space for corporate influence has widened. Private consultants are now routinely brought in to perform essential planning functions once located in the state. Often, these consultants come from firms whose alumni occupy key positions in government. The web of influence is dense, opaque, and largely unaccountable.

Corruption has become one of the dominant lenses through which South African political life is understood. Yet this discourse is often shaped by a narrow set of voices — NGOs, thinktanks, and donor-funded institutions — that speak as civil society but are frequently disconnected from the daily realities of working-class life.

Many of these organisations have done important work exposing malfeasance. But too often, their framing of corruption has been technocratic and depoliticised, focused on transparency and accountability in the abstract while avoiding deeper questions about inequality, power, and political economy. The systemic dimensions of corruption — including the role of neoliberalism, outsourcing, and elite patronage networks — are sidelined in favour of superficial metrics and compliance frameworks. Moreover, some of the leading white figures in this network have a tin ear when it comes to race, and some speak and write in ways that offend many if not most Black people.

This has limited the capacity of anti-corruption discourse to resonate widely. Many of the leading NGOs in this space are themselves reliant on international donors whose agendas are shaped by geopolitical priorities rather than grassroots realities. The result is a language of moral condemnation — often racialised — rather than popular and progressive political mobilisation, and one that struggles to confront the structural conditions in which corruption thrives.

Moreover, the NGOs' framing of corruption rarely accounts for the complicity of elite private actors — from multinational corporations to domestic capital — in sustaining the systems of extraction and inequality that underpin the crisis. Nor does it engage with how anti-corruption rhetoric can be weaponised to delegitimise state-led transformation or protect the status quo.

If South Africa is to build an effective and enduring response to corruption, it cannot rely solely on elite NGOs or donor-driven campaigns. What is needed is a genuinely popular and democratic left project — one that confronts the social and economic roots of corruption and reimagines the state as a vehicle for collective freedom.

CHAPTER 3

Poverty and Inequality

South Africa is often described as the most unequal country in the world. That inequality is not a historical accident, a policy failure, or the slow residue of a fading past. It is the product of a political settlement that reconfigured — but did not dismantle — a system of racial capitalism. As Sampie Terreblanche argued with devastating clarity, the transition to democracy was shaped by elite negotiations that protected white economic interests and incorporated a small Black elite into circuits of capital and state power. The result was not liberation but co-optation. The old order was not overturned. It was modernised.

To understand this, we must begin with the nature of the system itself. Capitalism in South Africa was forged through racial dispossession, super-exploitation, and the systematic denial of social and political rights to the majority. This was not a case of racism distorting capitalism — racism was constitutive of capitalism's functioning. In the words of Robin D.G. Kelley, racial capitalism is not a fusion of two systems, but a single, historically specific formation in which race is integral to value extraction. Kelley traces this tradition through Cedric Robinson and W.E.B. Du Bois, but, as he notes, it was theorised independently by South African Marxists in the 1970s.

It was Martin Legassick and David Hemson, working in the tradition of historical materialism, who argued that apartheid was not a relic of settler feudalism or a contradiction to capitalist modernity, but a necessary infrastructure for the reproduction of capital. The migrant labour system, influx control, the homelands, and the segregation of education and services were all designed to maintain a vast, cheap, and tightly controlled Black working class. The political superstructure of apartheid served the economic base of capital accumulation.

This insight has profound implications. It means that the end of apartheid did not, on its own, constitute a rupture with capitalism's racial foundations. As Terreblanche put it, the transition produced a "democracy of a special type" — one that allowed for the deracialisation of political representation and elite ownership, while leaving intact the deep structures of inequality, dispossession, and accumulation.

What emerged after 1994 was not a break with racial capitalism but its rebranding. The ANC, under the pressure of both international capital and domestic business, accepted a negotiated compromise that retained private property, entrenched the sanctity of contracts, and adopted a macroeconomic framework in line with neoliberal orthodoxy. The result was the political enfranchisement of the majority, coupled with their continued economic exclusion.

Over time, a new class formation has emerged. Poverty in South Africa remains overwhelmingly Black, and the working class continues to suffer under conditions of profound precarity, unemployment, and social abandonment. But the elite and the middle class have become significantly deracialised, and the super-elite is now majority Black. This reflects a limited and distorted form of transformation — one that offers upward mobility for the few while leaving the many behind.

The story told in much of mainstream political discourse is one of gradual progress, of democratic consolidation and racial inclusion. But the lived experience of most South Africans — especially young people, informal workers, the unemployed and the landless — tells a different story. It is a story of disillusionment, of promises deferred, and of dignity denied. It is a story in which democracy has come to mean the right to vote in a system that delivers exclusion, repression, and hunger. It is unsurprising that a majority of young people no longer bother to vote. Only 15% of eligible voters aged 18 to 21 registered for the 2021 election.

The Structure of Inequality: Wealth, Race, and Class

South Africa remains one of the most unequal societies on the planet. The Gini coefficient, which measures income inequality, consistently places the country at or near the top of global rankings. But income is only part of the story. Wealth inequality is even more extreme. A 2022 report by the World Bank estimated that the richest 10% of South Africans control more than 85% of household wealth, while the bottom 50% own virtually nothing. Within this landscape, poverty is racialised, gendered, and deeply spatialised.

The end of apartheid brought the vote, but not redistribution. Economic power — in the form of land, capital, and productive assets — has remained concentrated in a narrow segment of society. White South Africans, who make up less than 8% of the population, continued to control the lion's share of inherited wealth, corporate ownership, and high-income employment. The majority of Black South Africans, particularly those in working-class and rural communities, remained structurally locked out of wealth accumulation.

Yet this is not a simple binary between Black poverty and white wealth. The emergence of a Black elite, shaped through mechanisms like BEE, tender-based accumulation, and senior positions in the state and private sector, has created a new economic stratum — one that is politically connected, socially mobile, and increasingly powerful. The result is that the elite and the middle class have become significantly deracialised, even as poverty has remained overwhelmingly Black. South Africa's class structure has shifted: it is no longer a society divided only by race, but by a highly unequal and unstable class formation.

This elite incorporation has often been presented as evidence of progress. But it has also functioned as a mechanism of pacification. By creating avenues for upward mobility for the few, it has helped stabilise a system that remains fundamentally unjust. As Gumede and others have argued, BEE was quickly captured by political elites and turned into a tool for crony enrichment rather than broad-based empowerment. In many instances, "empowerment" became a euphemism for accumulation through the state — not through production or innovation, but through access to procurement contracts and regulatory favour.

Meanwhile, the lives of the majority have remained marked by unemployment, informal work, precarious shelter, and social abandonment. The unemployment rate among Black youth remains staggeringly high, often exceeding 60%, depending on how it is measured. Social grants provide a critical lifeline but are not a substitute for structural inclusion. Millions live in informal settlements, without secure tenure or adequate services. The promise of "a better life for all" has become a daily struggle for survival.

Spatial inequality also remains entrenched. The divide between rural and urban South Africa reflects not only uneven development, but a deeper legacy of dispossession. Land — perhaps the most symbolic and material site of apartheid injustice — remains unequally distributed, with large portions still in white hands, and much of the "redistributed" land under state custodianship or subject to bureaucratic dysfunction. In urban areas, housing policy has often reinforced apartheid geographies, pushing poor and working-class communities to the periphery, far from work, schools, and healthcare. The geography of apartheid has not been undone — it has been concretised in new forms.

This pattern of inequality is not static. It is dynamic, reproductive, and actively maintained. Economic policy continues to prioritise market confidence over social equity. The fiscal architecture of the state remains tethered to austerity. Public institutions, instead of functioning as engines of redistribution, often act as sites of capture and accumulation — reinforcing rather than resolving inequality.

At the same time, inequality is normalised in public discourse. The myth of meritocracy — that anyone can succeed through hard work — is repeatedly invoked to explain away structural exclusion. Blame is shifted to the poor themselves: for being "unemployable", for having too many children, for lacking entrepreneurial spirit. The problem is never the system — it is always the individual.

Perhaps the most crass example is Shauwn Mkhize, whose vast and extravagant wealth — luxury mansions, fleets of sports cars, a large arsenal of military-grade weapons, and the most expensive designer clothes — has been paraded across television screens and social media. Despite longstanding allegations of corruption linked to tender fraud, tax evasion, and worse, Mkhize has become a celebrity and reality TV star, the face of opulence in a society racked by poverty. Her story is treated as a model of success to be envied and emulated.

This normalisation of elite enrichment, even when rooted in brazen public theft at a staggering scale, is deeply revealing. It speaks to a society where wealth is increasingly detached from ethics, and where the spectacle of consumption is valued more than the means by which wealth was attained. In a country where millions go hungry, we admire and celebrate those who eat the most — even when they feast on public funds.

Moreover, the emerging elite formation has become increasingly criminalised and mafia-like, merging political power with organised extraction and violence. One example of this is the scandal surrounding Vusimuzi "Cat" Matlala, a tenderpreneur who infamously secured a R360 million South African Police Service health services contract, despite having no relevant experience and while already flagged for corruption. His company, Medicare24 Tshwane District, failed to deliver services but funded Matlala's lavish lifestyle — Rolls-Royces, mansions, expensive watches — while he maintained close protection from senior police figures.

Matlala's entanglement with the Tembisa Hospital corruption network, exposed by whistleblower Babita Deokaran, linked him to nearly R3 billion in suspect payments. Her murder in 2021 preceded wider revelations of syndicate politics and tender fraud. In May 2025, Matlala was arrested on charges including attempted murder and conspiracy, after allegedly orchestrating a hit on his former partner, actress Tebogo Thobejane — ordering that she be shot "in the face so that her family does not recognise her".

This kind of mafia politics, rooted in the capture of public institutions and enforced through violence, has played a contradictory role in the post-apartheid economy. On one hand, it produces Black wealth — ostentatious, politically protected, and often paraded as proof of transformation. It contributes to the deracialisation of elite status, offering the spectacle of Black success in luxury cars and mansions, secured through access to tenders and state-linked contracts.

But on the other hand, because this wealth is predatory on public resources — siphoned from hospitals, schools, housing budgets, and essential services — it simultaneously produces Black poverty. The very mechanisms that enrich a few actively deepen the immiseration of the many. This is not a redistribution of wealth from old white elites to new Black elites. It is a redistribution within Black communities. As public wealth is plundered for private enrichment it is seized from the poor majority by a powerful politically connected elite.

In this terrain, inequality no longer unfolds through bureaucratic order alone. It is reproduced through violence, assassinations, and structural capture, where political mobility is often criminal mobility — and the enrichment of the elite is bought with public debt and social abandonment.

From the RDP to Gear

In the first years after apartheid, there was a real sense that South Africa stood at the threshold of something new. The peaceful transition, the release of Nelson

Mandela, and the first democratic elections were experienced by many with a profound sense of hope. The world celebrated the "miracle" of South Africa's negotiated settlement, and liberal commentators spoke breathlessly of a Rainbow Nation being born. But the symbolism of racial reconciliation and the language of unity were quickly deployed to obscure the material foundations of inequality. The old order had been politically dethroned, but economically preserved.

Liberal narratives of transition focused on rights, votes, and inclusion into a legal framework. But this was a model of democracy emptied of redistribution. Structural inequality, rooted in centuries of land dispossession, cheap labour, and spatial segregation, was reframed not as a political and economic injustice requiring transformation, but as a technical problem to be managed. In this liberal framework, poverty became a technocratic question, often framed around 'service delivery'. Political struggle was abandoned in favour of technocratic policy implementation.

Nowhere was the liberal turn more evident than in the shift from the Reconstruction and Development Programme (RDP) to the Growth, Employment and Redistribution strategy (Gear). The RDP had been rooted, at least rhetorically, in the idea of redress — redistribution, land reform, mass housing, and free education. But Gear, adopted in 1996 without consultation, marked a sharp turn to neoliberal orthodoxy: fiscal austerity, inflation targeting, the privatisation of public assets, and a fixation on foreign investment. The state was restructured around the imperative of "macroeconomic stability", and social spending was increasingly subject to budgetary restraint. Redistribution was replaced by trickle-down hope.

In this reconfiguration, "delivery" replaced participation. Communities were invited to wait patiently for service rollouts, not to organise politically for structural change. Bureaucratic logics replaced democratic ones. Citizens were recast as clients. Protest was delegitimised as irrational and often seen as the result of an external conspiracy. The state's social contract became transactional — measured in kilolitres of water, housing units, and clinic visits — while the broader question of justice faded from view.

A whole academic and NGO industry followed this logic, as did much of the media. Unfortunately, much of the left academy also adopted a technocratic orientation to economics — one that largely sidestepped the deeper question of politics and power. Many implicitly positioned themselves not as agents of popular mobilisation but as more capable technocrats, seeking better policy outcomes without challenging the structures of elite authority or advancing democratic forms of mass power.

This liberal consensus, forged in the 1990s, shaped political life for more than a decade, entrenching a depoliticised and technocratic understanding of poverty. It has promoted the idea that inequality is the result of poor planning or corruption rather than the outcome of structural power. And it has enabled a system in which wealth remains radically unequally distributed, while the terms of that inequality — and the assumptions beneath it — go largely unchallenged in elite discourse.

It was only in 2005, with the emergence in Durban of an organised social movement from the wider Rebellion of the Poor that had begun the previous year, that poverty began to be directly politicised from below.

Governing Inequality

As poverty deepened after 1994, the democratic state increasingly came to govern inequality not by resolving it, but by managing and containing its effects. Nowhere is this more evident than in the expansive system of social grants. South Africa has one of the most extensive social protection systems in the Global South, with over 27 million people — nearly half the population — receiving some form of state support. These grants have unquestionably kept millions from absolute destitution. But they have also served to stabilise a deeply unjust system, creating a form of political pacification that dampens dissent without enabling real change.

Existing grants are modest and carefully rationed. They offer survival, not upliftment. Despite mounting calls from civil society and academic researchers, successive governments have resisted implementing a universal basic income grant. International experience suggests such a measure could significantly reduce poverty and restore a sense of agency and dignity to those locked out of the economy.

Instead, the prevailing logic has been one of minimal relief — a safety net that keeps people from falling into starvation but does little to alter the structure of exclusion. These grants should not be discarded, but expanded and universalised to form the basis of a genuine social safety net.

Rather than transforming inequality, the post-apartheid state has largely governed it through bureaucratic instruments — grants, rationed services, housing lists — and through local political structures that often function as instruments of control rather than empowerment. The ward councillor system, for example, was presented as a form of local democracy.

But in practice, it has frequently become a site of political patronage, dominated by local party structures rather than genuine community accountability. Councillors often operate as gatekeepers to scarce resources and opportunities, allocating housing, food parcels, jobs, and favours in ways that reproduce dependency and political loyalty. In some communities, access to services is mediated through alignment with local elites or party networks, not citizenship rights.

In many cases, ward councillors are not simply local bureaucrats — they are armed political actors. In provinces like KwaZulu-Natal and the Eastern Cape, ward councillors are often involved in violent competition over tenders and patronage networks. Assassinations are common. Local politics is not just contested; it is deadly. The ward councillor system has not brought democracy to the grassroots — it has brought political rivalry, coercion, and violence into everyday life.

Over time, local government has collapsed into dysfunction and capture. In many municipalities, basic services have broken down entirely — refuse goes uncollected, water is undrinkable, roads are cratered, and clinics barely function. What was once promised as developmental local government has become, in much of the country, a vehicle for elite extraction through tenders, contracts, and nepotism. The language of 'service delivery' has become detached from any meaningful social transformation. Instead, the local state has been hollowed out, repurposed as a site of accumulation for party-connected actors.

The rise of the tender state has compounded this crisis. Public procurement — once meant to serve the common good — has become one of the primary routes for elite enrichment. Contracts are inflated, services are undelivered, and institutions are gutted in the name of transformation. The logic of tenders creates incentives for proximity to power and not for quality, efficiency, or redistribution. It is a system that rewards loyalty, not competence. The result is a public sector that bleeds money but struggles to provide even the most basic services. Infrastructure collapses, but the politically connected thrive.

In this landscape, poverty is no longer an aberration to be eradicated; it is a condition to be administered. The poor are not treated as rights-bearing citizens but as a population to be governed — managed through grants, contained through patronage, and pacified through symbolic gestures. State legitimacy is increasingly maintained not through meaningful inclusion or democratic participation, but through control: who receives what, when, and on what terms.

This governing logic has produced a society in which rights are hollowed out and where mass unemployment is normalised, not addressed. Bureaucratic metrics substitute for justice, and political loyalty is more valuable than public accountability. As the social fabric frays, the language of service and transformation rings increasingly hollow.

Grassroots struggle has sustained a challenge to this mode of governance — not only confronting the state, but also compelling intellectuals and academics to reconsider how poverty is understood. Instead of accepting the technocratic logic that governs poverty through metrics and programmes, grassroots activists have insisted that poverty must be politicised, that it is rooted in land dispossession, systemic exclusion, and elite theft. They have rejected the reduction of the poor to passive recipients of charity or policy. In place of this, they have built a politics grounded in land, dignity, and collective self-organisation — asserting that the poor are not a population to be governed, but political actors with the right to shape their own futures.

Poverty and Patronage

Poverty is not only endured — it is administered, manipulated, and weaponised. At the local level, the experience of poverty is shaped less by the abstraction of policy and more by the everyday realities of gatekeeping, favour-trading, and clientelism. This is a world where survival often depends on political proximity, and where state resources intended to alleviate suffering are routinely deployed to secure loyalty, entrench control, and reproduce inequality.

The local state — particularly through the ward councillor system — has become central to the governance of poverty. Far from functioning as genuine democratic representatives, ward councillors are frequently the gatekeepers to critical resources such as food parcels, housing allocations, temporary jobs, and social relief. Access to these resources is often conditional, mediated through political allegiance to the ruling party or alignment with local power brokers. Those who dissent or stand outside the dominant patronage network may find themselves excluded, punished, or stigmatised.

In many communities, food parcels and housing lists are not neutral instruments of social relief — they are instruments of political mobilisation. Elections bring with them a flurry of activity as politicians and councillors distribute handouts in exchange for votes or promise service delivery on the condition of loyalty. This practice, widely referred to as "food for votes", is not new, but its brazenness has increased in recent years as the ruling party's legitimacy continues to erode. In such contexts, the right to basic necessities becomes a transactional affair. Support is rewarded; dissent is penalised.

Social grants, too, become part of this logic. What should be a universal right can become a contingent favour, dispensed or withheld to consolidate control.

Clientelism is not confined to the ruling party or to formal institutions. It extends into local networks of influence — civic associations, community leaders, traditional authorities — which often operate as intermediaries between the poor and the state. These actors can act as brokers of opportunity or instruments of coercion, depending on their alignment with formal power. In some rural areas, this system is reinforced by the authority of traditional leaders, who control land access and, in some cases, social development initiatives, often bypassing democratic processes altogether.

In urban townships and informal settlements, where party structures dominate local life, community meetings, protests, and development forums are often closely monitored or directly controlled by ward councillors or party activists. Independent organising is routinely repressed or delegitimised. The language of 'service delivery' masks a deeper reality: the local state has become a battlefield, where patronage, not justice, decides who eats, who works, and who waits.

This has profound consequences for political life. Democratic citizenship — the idea that every person has equal standing and rights — has been hollowed out in practice. People do not experience the state as a rights-bearing institution; they experience it as a fragmented and unreliable apparatus, mediated by local bosses and conditioned by loyalty. Protest, when it arises, is often met with repression, co-option, or violence. The line between the political and the criminal is increasingly blurred.

In this terrain, poverty is governed through relationships of dependency and fear. It is not merely the absence of income or employment; it is a condition of subjection to local hierarchies that thrive on scarcity.

And yet, despite this repressive machinery, resistance has not disappeared. It has taken different forms — quiet refusals, acts of non-cooperation, spontaneous protests, and, at times, organised defiance. But the cost is high. In a system where basic survival is conditional on loyalty, any assertion of autonomy is a political and personal risk.

Unemployment and Despair

The sheer scale of unemployment in South Africa is a structural and political emergency. The country has one of the highest unemployment rates in the world, with youth unemployment consistently exceeding 60%. This is not merely a matter of poor policy or economic mismanagement — it is the result of a long-term failure to build an inclusive economy. For millions of young people, particularly those in working-class and impoverished communities, the promise of democratic freedom has not translated into any material opportunity or stability. The result is a generation structurally locked out of formal employment and with no path to upward mobility.

The social and psychological costs of this mass unemployment are devastating. Communities are increasingly marked by despair — visible in widespread depression, hopelessness, and a corrosive sense of being unwanted or disposable. In this vacuum, destructive coping mechanisms take root. Drug use, including widespread use of heroin known as 'nyaope' or 'whoonga', has become endemic in some areas, particularly among unemployed young men.

The myths that surround these substances — such as the false claim that they are made from a mixture of rat poison and ARVs — do not reflect chemical truth but rather express a deep hostility to poor people. These myths are not just misinformed; they are anti-poor, blaming and dehumanising the most marginalised rather than addressing the structural causes of despair.

This despair often spills into anger, but with no progressive political direction, it is easily captured by reactionary forces. Xenophobia has become one of the most dangerous expressions of this trend — fuelled not only by political opportunists and demagogues, but also by the state itself. It is no coincidence that many of the most violent attacks on migrants have occurred in contexts of extreme unemployment and competition for scarce public resources. At the same time, gangsterism

— particularly in urban areas like the Cape Flats — offers young people a distorted but real form of belonging, income, and status in the absence of any viable alternatives.

The politics of despair is not just a symptom of exclusion; it is becoming a dominant mode of political life for many. The state has largely abandoned any serious strategy to address structural unemployment, and the ANC has shown little interest in rebuilding a productive economy capable of generating mass employment. Instead, the vacuum is filled with fear, scapegoating, and cycles of violence — a social crisis managed through repression, not resolution.

CHAPTER 4

Political Repression in Post-Apartheid South Africa

On 21 March 1960, apartheid police opened fire on a peaceful anti-pass protest in Sharpeville, killing 69 people and wounding more than 180. The Sharpeville Massacre shocked the world and ended any illusions about the legitimacy of South Africa's racial order. Over five decades later, on 16 August 2012, a democratic South African government ordered police to open fire on striking mineworkers at Marikana. Thirty-four workers were killed. This massacre — carried out in broad daylight, recorded on camera, and defended by state officials — shattered the international image of post-apartheid South Africa as a model democracy. It marked the moment when the reality of repression could no longer be denied or obscured.

If Sharpeville exposed the moral bankruptcy of apartheid, Marikana revealed the authoritarian core of a post-apartheid order that had aligned itself with capital and turned against the poor. The democratic state no longer simply failed to meet the expectations of the people — it actively criminalised and suppressed those who made political demands from below. Police bullets now defended profit, not apartheid, but the outcome was brutally familiar.

The massacre was not an aberration. As Julian Brown and others have shown, it was the outcome of a deeper political logic: the consolidation of a state willing to use violence to manage popular discontent and defend elite interests. Since 1994, political repression has never disappeared — it has been reorganised. Its language has changed, but its function remains: to contain, delegitimise, and often eliminate dissent that emerges outside of elite consensus.

The Marikana massacre was not the first instance of police violence in post-apartheid South Africa — but it was the moment when the state's willingness to kill in defence of capital was broadcast to the world. In the years leading up to 2012, poor communities had already endured waves of repression: evictions enforced at gunpoint, strikes broken by rubber bullets, activists arrested and tortured. But Marikana marked a decisive rupture. It was a public execution of striking workers, captured on film, carried out in broad daylight, and immediately defended by the state.

What made Marikana different was not only the scale of its brutality, but also its political clarity. It revealed that the post-apartheid order could and would deploy lethal force to protect corporate interests — in this case, a British mining firm — against its own citizens. The illusion of a neutral state committed to democratic mediation was shattered. The massacre forced a reckoning. Across South Africa and beyond, it became clear that the state was not merely failing to deliver justice to the poor — it was willing to kill to preserve the status quo.

In his study of the events, Brown argues that Marikana reflected a longer arc of securitisation, in which popular dissent had increasingly been framed as a threat to public order. Under the guise of "stability", the logic of counterinsurgency — once used against the liberation movement — had been redirected against poor and working class people. The massacre was not an aberration; it was the culmination of a trajectory that had been building over years of strikes, land occupations, and township revolts.

After Marikana, it became harder to sustain the moral prestige of the post-apartheid state. The language of reconciliation rang hollow in the face of the murdered miners. For many on the margins, the massacre confirmed what they had long experienced — that those who resisted exploitation could be treated as enemies of the state.

The Logic of Paranoia

By the time of the Marikana Massacre in 2012, the state's attitude towards grassroots dissent had already been shaped by a deep and growing paranoia — a conviction that popular organisation outside the ruling party was necessarily suspect, and likely manipulated by foreign or hostile forces. Marikana was not the beginning of this paranoia; it was its culmination. The willingness to use lethal force against striking mineworkers confirmed how deeply this logic had become embedded in the security establishment and political elite.

This tendency had been visible for more than a decade. In the early 2000s, the Treatment Action Campaign, which organised around access to antiretroviral medication during the AIDS pandemic, was accused by senior ANC officials of being funded by foreign governments to destabilise the state. One of the most militant of the earliest grassroots formations, the Western Cape Anti-Eviction Campaign, which organised against evictions, disconnections, and localised repression, was similarly maligned. In 2005, when Abahlali baseMjondolo emerged as a powerful voice for the dignity and democratic participation of shack dwellers, its members were branded "counter-revolutionary" and accused of being manipulated by an unnamed foreign government or a white academic — even though it was built by Black working class people from below.

This discursive attack was not incidental. The claim that grassroots movements were "third force" actors allowed the state to rationalise repression. In 2009, when armed men attacked Abahlali baseMjondolo in the Kennedy Road settlement in Durban, killing and displacing members of the movement, senior ANC figures initially celebrated the assault. Willies Mchunu, at the time MEC for transport, gleefully declared that the settlement had been "liberated". No one was held accountable. In the months that followed, police raids, arrests, and threats forced the movement underground.

Yet rather than being condemned, the repression was implicitly sanctioned by the state through its silence, and at times through explicit public support.

There was a relentless assumption — not only in the state, but also in significant parts of the NGO sector, the academy, and the media — that Black dissent must be the result of a conspiracy by malicious white actors. The possibility that Black people could organise themselves, on their own terms, outside elite scripts, was consistently denied.

This failure to recognise the political agency of the poor was perhaps most damaging on the left, particularly among some of the better-known figures in the middle-class networks connecting NGOs and the academy. Some went so far as to present Black grassroots activists who asked to be engaged with respect in criminal terms. Rather than recognise popular movements as political formations, they were often treated as disruptive, unruly, naïve, and ignorant. Just as with the state, there was a relentless assumption that grassroots Black activists who did not accept NGO and academic control must be under the control of a malicious white actor.

The logic of paranoia persisted and deepened over the years. From grassroots social movements to the Marikana workers' committees, formations that emerged outside the party were subjected to surveillance and infiltration. Even under the Ramaphosa administration — widely seen as a corrective to the authoritarianism of the Zuma years — this suspicion of autonomous organising remained intact. When movements raised questions about corruption, state capture, or service failures, they were often accused of playing into the hands of imperialist interests or of being manipulated by opposition parties or international NGOs.

The underlying fear was clear: a genuine popular politics, rooted outside the state and outside the ruling party, posed an existential threat to the post-apartheid consensus. To suppress that threat, the ANC often preferred to cast community organising as dangerous, rather than engage with its demands. The accusation of foreign manipulation became a political weapon — not only against social movements, but also against whistleblowers, dissidents, and even investigative journalists.

The irony, of course, is that while grassroots organisations were vilified for building transnational alliances or receiving small international grants, the South African government was itself deeply embedded in global networks of capital and reliant on foreign investment. The foreign "influence" that animated elite paranoia was always selective. A shack dweller reading Fanon or building links with movements in Brazil was suspect. A mining house headquartered in London or a development loan from the IMF was not.

Abahlali baseMjondolo: Dignity and Danger

Among the organisations that emerged in post-apartheid South Africa to contest inequality and exclusion, none has posed a more sustained or principled challenge than Abahlali baseMjondolo. Formed in 2005 following a protest organised in Durban's Kennedy Road settlement, the movement began with a simple demand: that the lives, intelligence, and dignity of poor Black people be taken seriously. From that demand grew a political vision rooted in land, housing, and democracy from below. What distinguished Abahlali was not just its autonomy from political parties and NGOs, but its insistence that shack dwellers speak for themselves, organise for themselves, and determine their own futures — in defiance of a system that insisted otherwise.

This insistence on dignity, land, and democratic self-organisation has come at a terrible cost. Abahlali has been subjected to waves of repression, often violent, sometimes fatal. From the outset, its autonomy and clarity of purpose provoked hostility from local political elites, and the movement was rapidly targeted by both state structures and party actors.

In September 2009, a vigilante mob aligned to local ANC structures launched a violent attack on Abahlali in the Kennedy Road settlement. Homes were destroyed, and several people were killed. Movement leaders were forced into hiding, and several members were arrested in what came to be known as the "Kennedy 12" case — later thrown out of court due to lack of evidence. The police not only failed to prevent the attack, but they also arrested the victims. No one from the attacking mob was held accountable.

The violence of the attack was not a one-off. It signalled a broader pattern: wherever the movement grew, repression followed. Members were subjected to unlawful evictions, harassment by local police, arbitrary arrests, and violent intimidation. More than once, leaders have been assassinated. In 2022, Lindokuhle Mnguni, the chairperson of the eKhenana Commune and a respected intellectual and organiser within the movement, was shot dead. He was the third senior Abahlali leader killed that year. His assassination followed a wave of arrests, including that of the movement's deputy president, George Bonono, and legal harassment against the commune's leadership. Mnguni's killing, like so many others, has gone unpunished.

Abahlali's enemies are not limited to the state. From early on, the movement challenged the often racialised paternalism of sections of the NGO sector and the academy. They insisted on being respected as political actors.

This refusal to accept NGO leadership infuriated some in civil society and resulted in intense hostility from a layer of self-appointed would-be leaders. Smear campaigns were launched, with movement leaders presented as criminals under the control of a malicious white actor. Abahlali's rejection of elite scripts — including the scripts of the left and liberal academy — made it a target not only for state violence, but also for intellectual delegitimation. The latter was often taken as legitimation for the former.

It was in this context that the movement's discourse of dignity acquired such force. Dignity was not an abstract idea. It was a practice founded in everyday struggles for decent shelter, for fair treatment at clinics and schools, for recognition in public discourse. To affirm the dignity of shack dwellers was, in this context, to reject the political and moral order that treated the urban poor as disposable.

Abahlali's political thinking, developed in part through its engagement with African traditions of communal life, offered a counter-vision to the dominant political imagination. It positioned the poorest South Africans not as a problem to be solved, but as protagonists in the struggle for a new society.

The movement's politics were both intensely local and sharply internationalist. While rooted in the immediate realities of informal settlements — mud, flooding, fire, hunger — Abahlali forged relationships with movements across Latin America and elsewhere in Africa. Its insistence on democratic organisation and collective land holding drew inspiration from the Brazilian Landless Workers' Movement (MST), and in turn inspired other groups across the continent.

This has not only unsettled the state. It has also disturbed the NGO-industrial complex and the South African academy, where many retain the unspoken assumption that Black grassroots organisers must operate under the direction of more educated or

professionalised actors. Abahlali's refusal of this logic —
and its refusal to be instrumentalised by parties or NGOs
— has been central to its enduring danger in the eyes of
the elite.

The state has responded with a combination of co-
optation, defamation, and brute force. While other
organisations have been contained via funding or
incorporated into official consultative processes,
Abahlali has consistently refused these overtures. As a
result, its members have been left exposed. While some
public intellectuals have defended the movement,
including figures from within the university system, the
broader intellectual establishment has often remained
silent in the face of serious repression. This silence is not
neutral. It is part of what allows the violence to continue.

At the time of writing, Abahlali has survived twenty
years of relentless repression and grown to become the
largest autonomous social movement in South Africa. Its
survival is remarkable. Its endurance is testimony to the
strength of its political vision, the commitment of its
organisers, and the resonance of its message among the
poor. But it is also a profound indictment of the South
African state — a state that has systematically treated
the democratic self-organisation of shack dwellers as a
threat, rather than as a legitimate expression of popular
sovereignty.

In a country where the language of rights is
everywhere, Abahlali has reminded us that rights
without power mean very little. In a country where
poverty is managed but not resolved, where protest is

criminalised and politics is reduced to technocratic delivery, Abahlali has affirmed the right to organise, to speak, and to think from below. It has done so at enormous cost. But in doing so, it has kept alive the possibility of a truly democratic future — one rooted not in elite bargains, but in the organised dignity of the excluded.

Rural Repression

Abahlali baseMjondolo is an urban movement — and, along with Brazil's MTST, one of the most significant urban movements in the world. However, the logic of repression is not limited to cities. Rural areas have also seen sustained and often lethal forms of repression, especially where communities have opposed mining projects and the local elite interests tied to them.

One of the best-known rural organisations is the Amadiba Crisis Committee, based in the Eastern Cape. It has long opposed attempts to impose titanium mining on the Wild Coast, a struggle that has met severe repression. In 2016, its chairperson, Sikhosiphi 'Bazooka' Rhadebe, was assassinated outside his home. The killing sent shockwaves through the country and the world and has never been resolved. Rhadebe was not only a community leader but a symbol of defiance against a nexus of interests involving the state, traditional authorities, and foreign mining capital.

Other rural land defenders have faced similar risks. In 2020, Fikile Ntshangase, a grandmother and respected environmental activist in KwaZulu-Natal, was assassinated in her home after opposing the expansion of a coal mine. She had refused to sign a compensation agreement and had vocally criticised the threats and intimidation being used to silence dissent. Her death marked a grim milestone in the escalating violence against those who challenge extractive projects in rural areas.

In many rural contexts, repression does not always come directly from the state. It is often enacted through traditional authorities aligned with mining companies and political elites, or by beneficiaries of Black economic empowerment deals who view community opposition as a threat to profit. The convergence of mining capital, local power brokers, and compromised governance has produced a hostile and dangerous terrain for grassroots activism.

Despite this, rural organisations continue to organise and resist, often in conditions of deep isolation and insecurity. They face smear campaigns, death threats, and accusations of being manipulated by foreign actors — the same playbook used against urban movements. But they persist, defending their land, communities, and democratic rights in the face of overwhelming odds.

This persistence is a powerful reminder that repression, while widespread, is never total. Even in the most marginalised areas, people continue to assert their right to say no, to organise, and to imagine different futures beyond extraction, corruption, and fear.

The Police

While political assassination has become an entrenched method of repression in post-apartheid South Africa — particularly in at the local level and struggles over land and tenders — the repressive machinery of the state also continues to operate through formal channels. The South African Police Service (SAPS) and the country's intelligence agencies have consistently been deployed to monitor, harass, and criminalise grassroots activists. This operates not only through violent encounters on the ground — especially in shack settlements and during protests — but also through more covert forms of repression, including illegal surveillance and political manipulation.

The SAPS has become increasingly militarised over the past two decades. Its approach to protests and popular dissent is often characterised by the use of disproportionate force — rubber bullets, tear gas, water cannon, and at times live ammunition. The perpetrators of this violence are rarely held accountable. In fact, police officers implicated in violent acts are routinely protected, and internal disciplinary systems are opaque, weak, or entirely inactive. This culture of impunity has allowed repressive policing to become entrenched.

Particularly in poor and working-class communities, the police often operate more like a force of occupation than an institution of public safety. Protest actions are regularly met with pre-emptive or retaliatory violence. Community leaders and movement organisers have been arrested and detained without cause, and sometimes tortured in custody. Activists have long reported illegal detentions, threats inside police stations, and trumped-up charges. In many cases, the police have been openly partisan — aligned with local political elites, especially in contexts where local ANC interests are threatened.

In recent years, police officers have also been directly implicated in political violence. There are credible allegations of police involvement in, or protection of, the perpetrators of politically motivated attacks, particularly in KwaZulu-Natal and parts of the Eastern Cape. When political killings occur, investigations are typically slow and often go nowhere. Where arrests are made, prosecutions seldom follow. In cases where activists have been killed, police have frequently failed to secure crime scenes, lost or ignored evidence, or shown open bias against the victims.

The state's intelligence services — including the State Security Agency (SSA) and various police intelligence divisions — continue to play a central role in repressing dissent. These agencies have engaged in unlawful surveillance of social movement leaders, unionists, critical academics, and journalists. In some cases, they have worked to infiltrate or destabilise grassroots organisations. The tools of Cold War counterinsurgency have been redirected not at armed enemies of the state, but at impoverished civilians demanding land, housing, and dignity.

The 2021 High-Level Review Panel on the SSA, chaired by Sydney Mufamadi, confirmed longstanding concerns about the politicisation of intelligence agencies. The panel found that resources had been misused to advance factional political interests and suppress dissent. Intelligence capabilities were frequently diverted towards domestic spying on activists, NGOs, and opposition voices. Despite these revelations, little structural reform has followed. The secretive nature of these agencies has shielded them from meaningful public scrutiny, and the line between intelligence work and political dirty tricks remains dangerously blurred.

In township and informal settlement contexts, policing is often experienced as arbitrary, corrupt, and violent. Communities report collusion between police and criminal syndicates, selective enforcement of the law, and widespread abuse of power. In many cases, community policing forums have failed to act as genuine oversight mechanisms, instead becoming captured by local elites or reduced to token consultation.

What emerges from all of this is a system in which the police and intelligence services do not serve the public equally, but rather act to defend particular interests — often political, economic, or criminal. Grassroots activists challenging local political elites, exposing corruption, or mobilising outside ANC patronage structures find themselves subjected to systematic forms of repression. The repressive capacities of the post-apartheid state have not disappeared; they have been repurposed.

Repression in post-apartheid South Africa is not an aberration. It is not simply the result of rogue actors, isolated incidents, or a deviation from an otherwise democratic norm. It is, rather, a systemic feature of how power is maintained in the present order. The use of repression — from overt violence and assassination to surveillance, intimidation, and political manipulation — serves a clear strategic function: to preserve elite accumulation, to maintain social control, and to foreclose the emergence of democratic alternatives from below.

The violence of the police, the surveillance of activists, and the assassinations of grassroots leaders are not merely symptoms of a dysfunctional state. They are often deliberate mechanisms through which specific political and economic interests are defended. Crucially, this is not about defending an old order, but about enabling new forms of elite accumulation — particularly those tied to mining, state contracts, and patronage networks. Repression often protects the interests of emerging elites whose wealth and power are directly linked to control over land, tenders, and local political structures.

The state represses the poor to defend property and political control — where "property" increasingly includes access to state resources, public contracts, and extractive deals. The repression is often most intense where insurgent popular democratic practices are most vibrant — in land occupations, self-organised movements, and worker committees that organise outside official union and party structures. These sites of autonomous political life represent a threat not because they are violent or illegitimate, but because they challenge the idea that political life must pass through party, state, or donor channels.

Repression also works ideologically. It casts dissent as criminal, foreign, manipulated, or naïve — anything but legitimate. It isolates grassroots activists from potential allies in civil society and academia. It replaces political dialogue with security logic. And it turns the pursuit of justice — for land, housing, and dignity — into a matter of law enforcement.

Ultimately, what emerges is a picture in which democratic rhetoric coexists with authoritarian practices. Constitutional rights are affirmed in law but denied in practice. Participatory processes are promised but often foreclosed through violence, co-option, or bureaucratic obstruction. In this environment, the line between state repression and criminal violence is frequently blurred, especially where state actors and local political elites intersect with business interests and shadowy networks of coercion.

The task is not only to document the logic of repression, but to insist on the legitimacy of popular struggle and to defend the space for democratic life to be built from below.

CHAPTER 5

Rising Fascism

The word fascism is often used loosely, as an insult or shorthand for any repressive political formation. But as every first-year politics student should know, fascism is a specific kind of far-right politics, defined by a core set of features. It is authoritarian, anti-democratic, and often militarised. It seeks to forge a single national identity by scapegoating and persecuting those deemed "other". It suppresses dissent and elevates the nation, the party, or the leader above the rule of law. And it replaces political pluralism with obedience, violence, and fear.

Fascism always targets the left. It seeks to discredit or destroy the people and organisations capable of organising collective resistance. Trade unions, grassroots movements, critical intellectuals, and popular organisations are attacked as traitors, saboteurs, or foreign agents. The aim is to prevent any challenge to the elite interests that fascism ultimately defends — by isolating dissenters and making examples of those who speak out.

Historically, fascism emerged in the twentieth century as a response to deep crises — economic depression, political deadlock, and fear of social revolution. In Italy, Germany, and Spain, fascist regimes promised national rebirth, unity, and order. In practice, they produced militarism, mass repression, and genocide. While fascism was defeated in its classic form by the end of the Second World War, it never disappeared. And today, under new conditions of economic breakdown, social fragmentation, and ecological collapse, it is returning — in new guises, and across a wider geography.

Fascism today is not only found in the margins or on the streets. It has entered government and mainstream politics in countries like India, where the Bharatiya Janata Party under Modi has fused Hindu nationalism, authoritarianism, and neoliberalism into a dangerously coherent political project. In Hungary and Turkey, authoritarian leaders have used state machinery to attack civil society, independent media, and minorities. In the United States, Donald Trump's rise brought openly racist, misogynistic, and conspiratorial politics into the heart of power, backed by violent movements and captured institutions. In Brazil, Jair Bolsonaro's presidency combined militarism, environmental destruction, and open nostalgia for dictatorship. And in Greece, Golden Dawn — a party with clear links to neo-Nazi ideology — briefly became the third-largest party before its criminal operations were exposed in court.

Each of these examples reflects a different path to power. But they share a logic: turning widespread despair, anger, and alienation into political energy through a process of misdirection. Instead of confronting the real sources of suffering — capitalist exploitation, elite corruption, and state failure — fascism tells people that their enemy is the vulnerable and marginal: the migrant, the dissident, the poor, the woman, the queer person. It replaces structural analysis with scapegoating, solidarity with suspicion, and democratic renewal with the fantasy of national purification.

In South Africa, these global dynamics are increasingly familiar. Our own post-apartheid order is in deep and undeniable crisis. The social gains of the early democratic period have been eroded. Mass unemployment, hunger, and infrastructural collapse are now part of daily life. The state has been hollowed out by corruption and political violence. The democratic centre has failed to deliver justice, dignity, or hope. And, in this vacuum, new political forces have emerged — many of them dangerous.

Some of these forces have adopted the language of the left, speaking of land, justice, and decolonisation. But closer scrutiny reveals that behind the rhetoric lies something else: authoritarianism, militarism, and elite enrichment. The language of radicalism is often used to mask deeply reactionary politics. The Economic Freedom Fighters (EFF), Black First Land First (BLF), and the uMkhonto weSizwe Party (MKP) have all incorporated aspects of fascist political culture — personality cults, violent rhetoric, suppression of dissent, and the scapegoating of enemies — into their political practice. Some have also directly aligned themselves with projects of kleptocracy, state capture, and repression.

But the clearest and most dangerous expression of contemporary fascism in South Africa is Operation

Dudula. A street-based collection of thugs in military uniform organised around the violent exclusion of migrants, Dudula has moved from vigilante actions to co-ordinated, large-scale campaigns of intimidation, social media propaganda, and institutional harassment. It operates with the language and imagery of militarised nationalism and it has often received informal support from elements of the police and state structures. Its rise has been met with disturbing silence — or even encouragement — from some corners of the political and media establishment.

The EFF's Authoritarian Populism

The first major political formation to emerge in post-apartheid South Africa with clearly fascist elements is the EFF. While the party is not itself a fascist formation, it has incorporated several aspects of fascist political culture into its practices — most notably militarism, authoritarianism, rhetorical volatility, and elite enrichment. These features have often been obscured by the party's left-wing rhetoric, particularly its emphasis on land redistribution, nationalisation, and anti-imperialism.

South Africa's commentariat, often poorly informed about political history, has tended to confuse left-sounding slogans with genuinely progressive politics. But, as history shows, fascism does not emerge only from the traditional right. Benito Mussolini himself came out of the socialist movement. The aesthetics, rhetoric, and even some of the policy gestures of the far right often mimic those of the left. In the absence of historical memory and political clarity, many observers mistake the EFF's rhetorical militancy for radical commitment. In reality, the party's politics have consistently aligned with authoritarianism and the enrichment of a new elite, rather than the building of democratic grassroots power.

The party's militaristic aesthetic is one of its defining features. EFF members wear red berets and uniforms, adopt military ranks and salutes, and march in formation at public events. Julius Malema, the party's leader, has fired a weapon at a rally. The party fosters a tightly controlled cult of personality around Malema, who dominates internal decision-making and public messaging. Dissent within the party has been repeatedly punished, and critics outside the party — especially journalists — have faced harassment and threats.

Despite its claims to represent the poor and marginalised, the EFF has not built meaningful grassroots structures or consistently supported popular struggles. Instead, the party has concentrated on parliamentary spectacle, media theatrics, and direct engagement with elite power. It has pursued an extremely effective media strategy, securing vastly more space in the public sphere than its electoral support would ordinarily justify. Its ability to dominate headlines and social media feeds has helped to mask its weak base and undemocratic practices.

The party's entanglement with elite corruption is well established. Malema's former company, On Point

Engineering, was awarded a lucrative tender to oversee infrastructure development in Limpopo province. Millions were siphoned off, and the company received payment to oversee the construction of a bridge that was never built. The EFF was also centrally implicated in the looting of VBS Mutual Bank, which collapsed in 2018, leaving working-class depositors in the lurch. These scandals revealed the EFF's role not as a force of redistribution, but as a vehicle for predatory forms of elite accumulation.

At times, the EFF has flirted with outright reactionary forms of politics. It has used xenophobic and anti-Indian rhetoric to incite public anger and present itself as the defender of the people. These gestures have been opportunistic — clearly attempting to incite resentment rather than simply reflect it — but they have not been sustained. The party has also, at times, adopted more principled pan-African positions on migration and solidarity. Its stance has oscillated between moments of opportunistic chauvinism and rhetorical internationalism, reflecting its tactical, rather than principled, orientation.

The EFF is a form of authoritarian populism. It mobilises the language of revolution while embracing centralised authority, personality cults, and violent rhetoric. Its attacks on journalists and critics, its closed internal structures, and well-documented corruption of its leaders all suggest the emergence of a political project that draws energy from public frustration — but offers no democratic or emancipatory path forward. The EFF is ultimately aligned with the predatory current within what Fanon called the national bourgeoisie. Its politics are marked not by a commitment to justice or equality, but by entanglement with the corruption of a new political elite in formation.

Black First Land First

Black First Land First (BLF) was never a political movement in any meaningful sense. It was a small, tightly controlled group — never more than a handful of individuals at any given time — with no grassroots base and no presence in workplaces, communities, or sites of popular struggle. Unlike classical fascist movements, which seek to mobilise mass support around authoritarian and ultra-nationalist ideas, BLF was essentially a media stunt. It used bombastic language, provocations, and conspiracy theories to generate headlines and controversy, but it had no capacity to organise or sustain any form of popular mobilisation. Its reach was wholly disproportionate to its size, thanks to its relentless courting of media attention and its ability to insert itself into public discourse through spectacle.

Nonetheless, its political orientation was unmistakably fascist. BLF adopted a racial-nationalist ideology rooted in the glorification of an imagined Black unity and the demonisation of perceived enemies. It sought to forge a paranoid and authoritarian political identity by combining racial essentialism with conspiratorial thinking and violent rhetoric. But this ideological posture was not in the service of any emancipatory project. On the contrary, it functioned as a shield for elite corruption and repression.

From its inception, BLF was closely aligned with the interests of Zuma and the Gupta family during the height of the state-capture project. It emerged as an instrument of political propaganda and disruption, offering its services to the most corrupt elements within the ruling elite. Its leader, Andile Mngxitama, had previously been expelled from the EFF and re-emerged as a vocal supporter of Zuma and the Guptas, defending their looting of the state under the banner of 'radical economic transformation'. BLF did not merely express sympathy — it actively defended the Guptas in public, and Mngxitama was found to have taken instructions from Bell Pottinger, the British PR firm hired by the Guptas.

The organisation attacked anyone who exposed or criticised this theft, from investigative journalists and civil society organisations to progressive academics and grassroots activists, which had long denounced Zuma's betrayal of the poor.

BLF recruited Bandile Mdlalose, a former Abahlali baseMjondolo member who had been expelled from the movement for gross corruption, and launched an online attack on the movement. Zuma has, farcically, always claimed to be 'pro-poor' – and the movement's strong critique of the ANC in general and Zuma in particular was an embarrassment to him and his project. BLF was deployed to discredit and intimidate the movement on his behalf. This is typical of the way fascism operates.

Alongside its propaganda work, BLF became a vehicle for the spread of conspiracy theories imported wholesale from the global far right. It promoted ideas about 5G technology causing Covid-19, repeated wild claims about Bill Gates and vaccine microchips, and embraced various forms of anti-science, and anti-democratic paranoia. This embrace of conspiratorial thinking, far from being a minor eccentricity, was central to its politics. Like fascist movements elsewhere, BLF used conspiracy to simplify the world into heroes and villains, to legitimise authoritarianism, and to distract from material realities like poverty, unemployment, and corruption.

It is an indictment of the weakness of the South African media that it allowed itself to be manipulated by a group as marginal as BLF. News outlets repeatedly platformed Mngxitama and treated the group as if it were a serious political force, despite its obvious lack of membership, grassroots work, or democratic practice. This failure played directly into BLF's strategy, giving a handful of provocateurs a national stage and amplifying its toxic politics.

In sum, BLF was a fascist project — defined by its authoritarianism, conspiracy, racial scapegoating, attacks on the left, and thuggish defence of elite looting. But it never became a fascist movement. It lacked mass appeal, grassroots structures, or real social roots. It was created in the image of its patrons: a political shell operation built to wage ideological warfare on behalf of kleptocrats. Its real legacy is not one of mass mobilisation or political transformation, but of distortion, intimidation, and the deliberate sabotage of democratic political discourse.

uMkhonto weSizwe Party

The uMkhonto weSizwe Party (MKP) is the most recent attempt by Zuma and his allies to reassert themselves on the national stage, drawing on nostalgia for the liberation struggle, exploiting ethnic loyalties, and cultivating a deeply authoritarian political culture. Its use of military uniforms, salutes, and general militaristic posture is designed to evoke the disciplined image of the original MK — the ANC's armed wing — while positioning itself as the custodian of a betrayed revolutionary legacy. In practice, it is a profoundly reactionary formation.

The MKP is deeply rooted in the collapse of the ANC's moral authority. As the ruling party has lost legitimacy, Zuma and his allies have moved to appropriate the symbols of struggle for their own political project. What the MKP offers is not a vision of transformation or justice, but a restorationist fantasy — a return to power for a discredited elite under the cover of historical symbolism. It is not a new political force in any meaningful ideological sense. It is a parasitic formation, recycling the language of liberation while aligning itself with some of the most corrosive elements of the post-apartheid order.

Unlike the EFF, which has struggled to build viable grassroots structures, the MKP is actively establishing vibrant branches, especially in KwaZulu-Natal. But these branches operate within a tightly controlled and authoritarian framework. There are no internal elections, no real mechanisms for debate, and no culture of democratic deliberation. Zuma exercises total control over the party, and internal discipline is maintained through expulsions, surveillance, and a culture of paranoia. The party leadership is centred around personal loyalty, and dissent is treated as betrayal. This is not a democratic formation in any meaningful sense.

The MKP thrives on spectacle — on rallies, marches, uniforms, and displays of strength. Its appeal is not grounded in programmes or principles, but in a combination of sentiment, intimidation, and performance. It seeks to project a sense of power and inevitability, tapping into fears of national collapse and fantasies of order restored through force. This performative politics has been particularly effective in areas where state institutions have broken down and loyalty to Zuma remains high.

The party's ideological orientation is murky but marked by consistent support for authoritarian and monarchical institutions. It has expressed strong backing for the Zulu monarchy and traditional leadership structures, as well as the absolute monarchy in Swaziland and even the regime in Morocco. Its public rhetoric is laced with ethnic chauvinism and extreme xenophobia. It offers no coherent political programme beyond resentment, retribution, and symbolic domination.

The MKP is not simply a populist reaction to national crisis—it is a deliberate project to rehabilitate the networks of corruption, repression, and elite patronage that defined the Zuma era. Its authoritarianism is not incidental. It is foundational.

Operation Dudula

Operation Dudula is the clearest fascist formation in South Africa today. Unlike those that merely flirt with authoritarian rhetoric, Dudula organises street-level vigilantism in military uniforms and direct action to violently exclude migrants and the poor under the guise of "putting South Africans first".

Dudula emerged from the collapse of municipal services, mass unemployment, and the erosion of state legitimacy. Instead of confronting systemic economic failure, it redirects rage towards foreign nationals — labelling them as criminals, invaders, and threats to national purity. This scapegoating masquerades as patriotism, giving vulnerable communities a false sense of empowerment while obscuring elite culpability.

The movement has carried out coordinated raids against foreign nationals: storming clinics, harassing health workers, blocking access for pregnant women, and forcibly evicting street traders. Such scenes have been shared widely on social media, both as spectacle and propaganda. Paid campaigns amplify xenophobic framing and smear critical voices — referring to migrants, activists, and community organisers as "traitors" or "sell-outs".

This hateful climate culminated in the brutal murder of Zimbabwean national Elvis Nyathi in Diepsloot on 6 April 2022. He was dragged from his home, beaten, and burned alive by a mob incited by xenophobic rhetoric. His murder stands as a stark warning of the deadly consequences of normalised hatred. No serious political response followed.

The media has played a significant role in legitimising Dudula. Its leaders have been given uncritical platforms to vent xenophobic bile, while those they target are made to account and defend themselves. This dynamic has helped shift the political centre, treating xenophobia as a legitimate position in national debate and not as the threat to democracy it is.

Dudula claims to speak for the poor. Yet the largest organisation of the poor in South Africa — Abahlali baseMjondolo, with more than 180,000 members — has categorically rejected this claim and condemned Dudula as a violent and fascist force that undermines the dignity of the poor and diverts attention from those truly responsible for poverty and social collapse. In two detailed press statements issued on 17 July 2025 and 21 July 2025, Abahlali denounced Dudula's actions as attacks on the poor, not a defence of them. The movement noted that genuine grassroots organisations fighting for dignity and justice have become targets of Dudula's wrath.

In response, Abahlali has faced an avalanche of open and grisly death threats from Dudula supporters — many issued publicly and in broad daylight. The threats are not only directed at individuals, but at the very principle of grassroots organising that refuses to scapegoat the vulnerable. The silence of the state in the face of these threats has been deafening.

Equally disturbing is the silence of major institutions of the left. None of the major trade union federations — Numsa, Saftu, or Cosatu — rallied to support Abahlali baseMjondolo on the streets, or even issued statements condemning Dudula. Neither did the South African Communist Party. This is not simply disappointing — it is disgraceful. The failure of these organisations to defend core democratic values and internationalist working-class solidarity in the face of a fascist formation signals a deep political crisis on the South African left. It should, though, be noted that, to his credit, Zwelinzima Vavi did later describe Abahlali baseMjondolo as "heroes" and affirm the position they took against Operation Dudula.

Elements within the police have tolerated or supported Dudula's actions, standing by during raids or even collaborating with their activities. Rather than confronting the violence, political figures across much of the centre have offered only muted or evasive responses.

Operation Dudula is no fringe phenomenon. It represents the naturalisation of fascist logic under conditions of institutional breakdown: scapegoating, violent spectacle, and impunity. Its growth signifies the failure of democratic institutions, media, and political leadership. Unless anxiety and desperation are redirected toward elites — instead of neighbours — fascist political formations will continue to find fertile ground.

The Electoral Normalisation of Xenophobia

In South Africa, as in much of the world, xenophobia has become a central pillar of fascist and proto-fascist politics. Mobilising resentment against migrants serves to redirect popular anger away from corrupt elites and collapsing institutions, and towards vulnerable people with even less power and fewer rights. It offers easy scapegoats for unemployment, crime, and decaying infrastructure — problems caused not by migration, but by the failures of the post-apartheid state and the predatory behaviour of the ruling class.

While street-based organisations like Operation Dudula have driven this politics from below, electoral parties have increasingly taken up xenophobic rhetoric from above, granting it a veneer of legitimacy. The turn to anti-migrant scapegoating in parliament and municipal councils mirrors global trends in which far-right ideologies creep into the mainstream, cloaked in the language of sovereignty, order, and community protection.

South Africa now has multiple openly xenophobic parties operating in formal politics, including the Patriotic Alliance (PA) and ActionSA. Their presence in coalition governments and municipal councils has given fascist-adjacent ideologies a foothold in public institutions and lawmaking. The PA, led by Gayton McKenzie, projects an image of "tough-on-crime" populism while stoking anti-migrant sentiment in impoverished communities. Its leadership, including individuals with serious criminal records, fuses ethno-populism, gangsterism, and anti-migrant scapegoating. The PA has, in effect, used xenophobia to deflect attention from its own entanglement in clientelism, corruption, and the looting of public funds.

ActionSA, led by Herman Mashaba, has followed a similar trajectory. As Johannesburg mayor, Mashaba repeatedly made inflammatory anti-migrant remarks, infamously stating that foreign nationals were "bringing us Ebola"—a statement that drew widespread condemnation but which also consolidated his image as a hardliner. His politics frames migrants as the source of social decay and economic instability, despite all evidence to the contrary. This brand of xenophobic populism has translated into measurable electoral support, enabling ActionSA to form part of local government coalitions.

Although the PA and ActionSA have adopted the most explicit anti-migrant postures, the rot is not confined to the political fringes. The ANC and DA have both, in different ways, legitimised elements of the turn to xenophobia. Senior ANC officials have repeatedly made public statements blaming undocumented migrants for service delivery failures, while the DA's Western Cape government has pursued raids and evictions targeting foreign nationals. The refusal of the political centre to draw a firm line has created a permissive environment in which xenophobic violence and policy proposals flourish without serious challenge.

In this climate, it is no longer fringe to call for mass deportations, to campaign on the promise of removing "foreigners", or to frame migration as a national security threat. Fascist logics — of purification, exclusion, and violent retribution — are seeping into the ordinary language of politics, often disguised as pragmatic responses to popular frustration. But this language obscures the structural causes of South Africa's social crisis, offering instead a dangerous and profoundly dishonest politics of scapegoating.

Why Fascism Now?

The emergence of fascist and proto-fascist formations in post-apartheid South Africa cannot be explained simply by reference to charismatic figures or opportunistic parties. It is a symptom of deeper crises: a long political, economic, and moral unravelling that has opened space for authoritarian and exclusionary politics.

South Africa's political centre has collapsed. The ANC's legitimacy has been profoundly eroded, not just by corruption and factionalism, but by its failure to address mass unemployment, land dispossession, deepening inequality, and the collapse of public services. At the same time, mass disillusionment with formal institutions has become endemic. For millions, the promises of democracy have not materialised. What remains is despair, resentment, and a growing openness to authoritarian solutions.

While grassroots struggles persist, there is no left parliamentary alternative. Many trade unions are either captured by donor networks or trapped in narrow party alliances that erode their independence. It is widely acknowledged that one of the most senior trade union leaders in the country is beholden to a funder.

The post-apartheid order failed to reckon with the enduring legacies of authoritarianism and violence embedded in the state and society. The negotiated transition prioritised elite pacts and reconciliation over structural transformation. Apartheid's bureaucratic and coercive apparatuses were not dismantled; they were renamed. Authoritarian features within the police, intelligence services, and even schooling, remained intact.

Simultaneously, the celebration of violence within the liberation movement — once directed against a justifiable enemy — was never adequately interrogated. It continued into the democratic era, helping to legitimise violent postures and masculinist forms of political expression. Today, fascist formations draw directly on this unresolved culture of authoritarianism and romanticised militarism.

Mainstream media institutions have played a deeply contradictory role. On one hand, they investigate corruption and give voice to dissent. On the other hand, they have consistently platformed reactionary voices and offered fascist and xenophobic figures uncritical exposure. In so doing, they legitimise bigotry by presenting it as just another "side" in a supposed national debate. Demagogues with no grassroots support are elevated, while democratic and poor people's struggles are marginalised or misrepresented. This failure has normalised the rhetoric of hate.

Neoliberalism has not just ravaged the material basis of social life — it has corroded the psychic and affective infrastructure of solidarity. It has created a world in which people are reduced to economic units, social bonds are shattered, and abandonment is the norm. This atomisation makes collective political action difficult to sustain. In the void, fascism steps in, offering not justice or liberation but identity, vengeance, and a sense of belonging. It satisfies emotional needs — humiliation, envy, anger — by directing them at scapegoats.

Fascist and proto-fascist movements also trade in masculinist fantasies. In a country where structural unemployment among young men is among the highest in the world, the loss of social role and economic autonomy has created widespread rage and humiliation. Militarism, uniforms, salutes, and the language of combat offer a fantasy of restored agency. These symbolic performances substitute for power, and in doing so, become powerful. They enable a theatre of domination in which the vulnerable feel momentarily strong.

South Africa's fascist currents do not exist in isolation. They are part of a global resurgence of the far right.

South African figures and organisations draw heavily on global reactionary narratives—from Covid denialism to anti-immigrant nationalism. Online propaganda and conspiracy theory networks transcend borders, helping to circulate memes, talking points, and aesthetic cues. Fascism today is transnational in culture, even if it is parochial in politics.

The elite consensus that underpinned the democratic transition was never rooted in mass participation. It was an agreement among elites, often viewed by the majority as imposed rather than chosen. Over time, that consensus has broken down. For elements of the post-apartheid elite, fascist politics now offers a means of retaining power by weaponising resentment. They seek to redirect popular anger away from capital and corruption and towards migrants, minorities, and the left. In doing so, they undermine democracy while claiming to speak for "the people".

Fascism has arrived at this moment because South Africa's dominant institutions — political, economic, and cultural — have failed. The state is hollowed out, the ANC is in terminal decline, and the public imagination is exhausted. Into that vacuum has stepped a volatile mix of opportunists, nostalgists, demagogues, and criminals, all seeking to mobilise rage for their own ends. Without a credible and popular alternative that can meet people's material and emotional needs — without life-affirming institutions, as Ruth Wilson Gilmore puts it — the forces of reaction will continue to grow.

CHAPTER 6

Violence and the Unmaking of the State

Earlier, we traced how the ANC became a party increasingly shaped by elite interests, unable or unwilling to address the core crises of mass impoverishment and rising authoritarianism. In this chapter, we turn to the violence that underpins this degeneration — violence that is not incidental to the post-apartheid order but central to it.

South Africa today has one of the highest murder rates in the world. In 2023, more than 27,000 people were killed — an average of 75 murders a day. While Honduras, El Salvador, Jamaica, and parts of Mexico have occasionally posted higher rates, South Africa consistently ranks in the top ten globally outside of active war zones. The scale of lethal violence is not only a national emergency. It is a sign of a profound breakdown in social order.

The long arc of the country's murder rate tells a revealing story. After apartheid, there was a steady but uneven decline in homicides — reaching a low during the latter part of Mbeki's presidency. But under Zuma, the numbers began to rise sharply again. By the time Ramaphosa took office, South Africa was facing a crisis of violence that continues to escalate.

This is not merely statistical. The experience of violence permeates daily life in many communities. Taxi wars, domestic violence, gang killings, vigilantism, and police shootings all contribute to an environment of chronic insecurity. The state has lost its monopoly on exercising force in many areas, while its capacity for protection and justice has been steadily hollowed out.

Alcohol plays a significant role in this pattern. Researchers and health professionals have consistently shown that a large proportion of murders in South Africa occur in contexts of heavy drinking. Binge drinking, often over weekends or at the end of the month, is closely correlated with spikes in interpersonal violence. Studies also highlight how alcohol exacerbates gender-based violence, adding to the burden on already strained policing and health systems.

The geography of violence is uneven but revealing. While rural areas and small towns are not immune, urban centres in provinces like the Western Cape, Eastern Cape, KwaZulu-Natal, and Gauteng show especially high murder rates. In Cape Town, neighbourhoods like Nyanga and Delft have become symbols of the crisis, with murder rates rivalling those of war-torn cities. In the Eastern Cape, gang-linked killings in towns like Mthatha and Gqeberha have reached alarming levels. In KwaZulu-Natal, murder intersects with political patronage, organised crime, and struggles over territory.

These high levels of violence reflect more than just crime. They reflect abandonment. The post-apartheid promise of transformation has failed to materialise for millions. Economic stagnation, youth unemployment, spatial marginalisation, and pervasive corruption have hollowed out the social contract. The state is no longer seen as a guarantor of order or justice. In some communities, gang leaders or taxi bosses are more feared — and often more effective — than the police.

The SAPS has been profoundly weakened. Chronic underfunding, politicised appointments, corruption, and demoralisation have crippled its ability to respond. Detection rates for murder remain shockingly low, and conviction rates are even lower. This impunity reinforces the perception that violence is both unavoidable and unpunishable.

South Africa's murder crisis is not simply a problem of policing. It is the mirror of a deeper crisis: the collapse of a shared moral order, the erosion of public trust, and the brutalisation of everyday life. The question is not just how many people are being killed, but what kind of society makes this level of killing possible.

Democracy and violence: lessons from Jamaica

We are not alone in suffering from such terrifying rates of violence. Orlando Patterson, the Jamaican-American sociologist and historical theorist, has offered a striking and controversial account of the high rates of violence in Jamaica. His work, drawing on decades of research and reflection, challenges common liberal assumptions that democracy is always accompanied by peace and order.

Instead, Patterson argues that under certain conditions — especially in deeply unequal, postcolonial societies — democracy can actually fuel violence rather than reduce it.

Patterson's central thesis is that in places like Jamaica, where poverty, inequality, and clientelism define much of political and social life, the introduction of electoral democracy in the absence of meaningful economic transformation created new forms of conflict and competition. Rather than producing a culture of negotiation and compromise, democratic processes became fused with violent forms of political rivalry. During Jamaica's post-independence period, political parties — especially the People's National Party and the Jamaica Labour Party — often relied on gangs and strongmen to secure voter loyalty in urban ghettos. This created a fusion between partisan politics and organised crime that persists today.

In this context, democratic competition did not reduce violence — it intensified it. In his work, Patterson points to the 1970s in Jamaica as a critical period, when electoral politics and gang violence became deeply intertwined, resulting in surges of murders during election years. At the heart of this dynamic is a form of patronage politics in which political leaders deliver scarce resources to their supporters, often via informal and coercive networks. In turn, young men in impoverished areas, excluded from formal employment and education, are pulled into political gangs that promise protection and opportunity — but also demand loyalty and violent enforcement of territorial boundaries.

This argument marks a significant departure from standard liberal political theory, which often assumes that violence precedes democracy and that democratic governance will gradually displace it. For Patterson, the failure to create economic inclusion and to dismantle colonial legacies meant that democracy did not bring peace, but restructured violence in new ways. In fact, he goes so far as to argue that under conditions of extreme inequality and weak institutions, democracy itself can deepen a sense of injustice. When people are promised rights, opportunities, and equality at the ballot box but denied them in everyday life, frustration and disillusionment often manifest in destructive ways.

The Jamaican case is thus not an isolated story of failed governance or corruption — it is a structural problem rooted in the legacy of slavery, colonialism, and uneven development. Violence in this context is not simply criminal. It is political, economic, and social. It is a way of navigating a system that has always excluded the majority.

There are powerful parallels with South Africa. Like Jamaica, South Africa is a postcolonial society with deep structural inequalities rooted in a brutal past. Like Jamaica, it has embraced formal democracy, with regular elections, a constitution, and civil liberties. But also like Jamaica, South Africa has failed to deliver on many of the material promises of democracy, particularly for poor and working-class people. Housing, land, education, and jobs remain out of reach for millions.

In South Africa, as in Jamaica, this has fuelled a crisis of legitimacy. Politicians use patronage networks to distribute state resources and access to opportunities. Local strongmen, often ward councillors or community leaders, control these flows. Violence becomes a tool for enforcing political loyalty or eliminating rivals. The killings of local councillors, grassroots political activists, whistleblowers, and union leaders in South Africa echo the same patterns Patterson identifies in Jamaica.

But there is a deeper resonance in Patterson's argument that democracy, under the wrong conditions, can generate its own forms of violence. In societies where the expectations of the democratic ideal — freedom, equality, justice — are systematically betrayed by the everyday realities of exclusion and degradation, democracy can generate deep resentment. And when formal institutions are weak, corrupt, or inaccessible, violence becomes a language through which grievances are expressed and claims are made.

Importantly, Patterson does not argue that democracy is inherently violent. Rather, he insists that without economic justice, strong institutions, and a culture of inclusion, democracy can become hollow — an empty ritual that masks brutal social realities. Under such conditions, people may vote, but they are also killing and being killed in the name of politics. Elections become sites of conflict, not peaceful competition.

Politics becomes inseparable from gangsterism. Violence becomes a way of doing politics.

In South Africa, where murder rates remain among the highest in the world, these insights are crucial. It is not enough to celebrate the procedural aspects of democracy. We must ask hard questions about what democracy means when it coexists with extreme poverty, corruption, and systemic violence. As in Jamaica, young men are often at the centre of this crisis — men who are unemployed, unsupported, and trapped in conditions of despair. Violence becomes one of the few available routes to power, respect, or even survival.

To understand this, we must go beyond the idea of violence as a breakdown of order. We must recognise it as part of the order itself — as a symptom of a system that offers dignity and opportunity to the few, and leaves the rest to fight for scraps. Patterson's work helps us see this not as a moral failing, but as a structural consequence of how democracy has been constructed in societies shaped by slavery, colonialism, and neoliberalism.

A crisis in policing

It is very common for South Africans to respond to terrifying levels of violence by asking for greater policing. However, the police themselves are frequently perpetrators of unlawful forms of violence.

The everyday operations of the police are marked by fatal shootings, torture, custodial rape, and political repression. This violence is not an aberration but a deeply entrenched feature of the post-apartheid order.

The statistics are stark. Between April 2023 and March 2024, the Independent Police Investigative Directorate (IPID) recorded 460 deaths due to police action. Of these, 212 occurred in custody. Serious assaults numbered over 3,100, with 273 cases of torture and more than 110 allegations of rape, including custodial rape — a figure that has increased by 75% in recent years. These figures are almost certainly underestimates, given the well-documented reluctance of victims to report abuse.

South African police are among the most lethal in the world, far outpacing their counterparts in the United States, Canada, and elsewhere. Paul T. Clarke notes that South Africa has one of the highest per capita rates of police killings globally, exceeding those in the United States. His analysis highlights the way in which police violence in South Africa is both extreme and normalised, directed overwhelmingly at the Black poor. He argues that rather than functioning as a protective service, the police operate as a mechanism of repression, targeting the marginalised through lethal force.

The killing of 16-year-old Nathaniel Julies in Eldorado Park in 2020, a child with Down syndrome shot dead by police, was a moment of national shock. But it was not an exception.

David Bruce, a former political prisoner now working as a researcher, has consistently argued that police brutality in South Africa is not a residual pathology left over from apartheid but an institutionalised feature of contemporary governance. In his words, "The use of excessive force is not a problem of a few "bad apples" but a routine part of everyday policing in many places across South Africa."

A key driver of this violence is the increasing militarisation of the police. This shift is visible in the deployment of Tactical Response Teams and the normalisation of shoot-to-kill rhetoric. KwaZulu-Natal's provincial police commissioner, Nhlanhla Mkhwanazi, has revived such language under the guise of a "war on criminals". The extraordinarily thoughtful public intellectual Malaika Mahlatsi interrogates this war, raising the question of whether it has come at the cost of South Africa's constitutional democracy, and notes the increasing number of extrajudicial executions carried out by the police in the province.

The 2012 Marikana massacre stands as a stark reminder of the state's willingness to meet protest with deadly force. Thirty-four striking mineworkers were shot dead by police in what remains the most lethal use of force against civilians in democratic South Africa. But Marikana is not the only case. In 2011, Andries Tatane was killed by police during a service delivery protest in Ficksburg. His death, captured on live television, exposed the violent response often meted out to grassroots dissent.

The repression of protest is widespread. Scores of protesters have been killed by police since the end of apartheid, often during community protests around basic services or housing. In 2011, Human Rights Watch documented 27 police-related deaths in 62 protest incidents. Grassroots movements have long documented unlawful arrests, assaults, and shootings during protests and evictions. The routine deployment of armoured vehicles and helicopters against unarmed shack dwellers speaks to a security logic that sees the poor not as citizens but as threats.

During the Covid-19 lockdown, police and army units were widely deployed to enforce regulations. This led to numerous incidents of abuse. In one case, Collins Khosa was beaten to death by members of the South African National Defence Force in his own yard. IPID recorded a spike in complaints against police officers during this period, many involving arbitrary force and humiliation.

This culture of violence is underwritten by a near-total lack of accountability. IPID, though mandated to investigate police misconduct, remains under-resourced and lacks prosecutorial power. In the same year that hundreds of serious assaults and dozens of deaths were reported, only 55 disciplinary convictions were secured. Of these, just 10 were for unlawful use of force. The failure to hold perpetrators accountable has bred a sense of impunity within the ranks of the police.

Police abuse also extends into the police stations and cells. Torture remains common, especially in the form of beatings and suffocation. Custodial rape, disproportionately affecting women and LGBTQ+ people, has surged. In some prisons, detainees have reported being shocked with electric wires, having plastic bags tied over their heads, or being suspended from the ceiling. Victims report being too afraid to come forward, fearing further violence or disbelief. The result is a systemic rot that corrodes trust in law enforcement.

Police violence in South Africa also takes on a xenophobic character. During waves of anti-immigrant violence, particularly in townships and informal settlements, police have often failed to intervene — or have actively participated in abuses against foreign nationals. Numerous reports, including those by Human Rights Watch and local civil society organisations, have documented arbitrary arrests, extortion, beatings, and even unlawful deportations targeting migrants, particularly those from other African countries. These actions are rarely investigated, reinforcing a message that violence against non-nationals is tolerated by law enforcement.

Sex workers also face routine harassment and abuse by the police. Studies and advocacy reports have consistently found that sex workers are frequently subjected to physical and sexual violence, extortion, and arbitrary detention. The criminalisation of sex work creates a context in which police act with impunity, knowing that victims are unlikely to report abuse for fear of arrest or stigma.

This violence not only targets poor and other vulnerable people. It is also deeply political. From the repression of protests and mass evictions to the surveillance of activists and the harassment of journalists, the state has increasingly used the police to manage dissent. In 2012, *Mail & Guardian* journalists were interrogated after reporting on corruption. These incidents point to the use of police as instruments of political control.

The echoes of apartheid are unmistakable. The apartheid-era Security Branch may be gone, but many of its tactics survive. Today's repression is more decentralised, less ideologically driven, but no less brutal. The police, in many poor communities, are not seen as protectors but as predators.

In some areas, residents report feeling safer under the authority of gangs than the police. The Khayelitsha Commission of Inquiry found a 363% increase in complaints against police officers in the area between 2009 and 2014, many involving extortion, arbitrary detention, and brutality. In such contexts, the state has lost not only legitimacy but the monopoly on violence.

This pattern is not unique to South Africa. In Brazil, police violence also disproportionately targets the Black poor, with thousands of people killed each year in favelas under the pretext of anti-crime operations. In Kenya, extrajudicial executions and disappearances have become a persistent feature of policing in poor communities. In each of these countries, the same dynamics are at play: a militarised, unaccountable police force used to contain the poor rather than serve and protect them.

As in several countries around the world, especially in Central America, crime and politics often intersect, with the result that political assassinations are common.

Once, assassination was a blunt instrument of apartheid — shaping political order through terror. Today, it fuels a privatised violence that defends predatory accumulation rather than ideology. The ideological mask has vanished; what remains is an economy governed by fear and contract death.

Political Assassinations

Violence has become a key mechanism through which access to state resources is regulated and defended. It is no longer only a tool of political control but also of economic accumulation.

This system of violence is not confined to any one province, but its intensity and visibility are concentrated in KwaZulu-Natal. Large numbers of councillors have been killed across the province, alongside activists, bureaucrats, and others. According to the Moerane Commission, set up to investigate political killings in KwaZulu-Natal, the problem had become systemic. It noted that violence was not only used to eliminate rivals, but also to enforce party discipline and settle internal scores. In the words of the commission, "Violence has become a means of pursuing political power".

The numbers are staggering. By 2021, David Bruce had recorded more than 450 politically linked assassinations since 2000. These include figures within the ANC, as well as community leaders, union organisers, and grassroots activists. The murder of officials tasked with ensuring accountability, such as municipal audit committee members, has become disturbingly common.

The line between party, state, and criminal enterprise has blurred. Corrupt tenders are defended through hitmen. Rivalry over positions — and the access to wealth they promise — has turned deadly. The police are often complicit or incapacitated. The assassins are rarely caught. As Bruce puts it, impunity is not a side-effect of the system; it is the system.

One of the most high-profile recent cases was the 2021 assassination of Gauteng health department official Babita Deokaran, who had flagged suspicious payments linked to politically connected businesspeople. But there are countless lesser-known examples. In 2020, police officer Charl Kinnear was assassinated while investigating extortion networks with alleged political protection. Grassroots activists, especially those resisting evictions, refusing to allow the extraction of rent from shack settlements, or exposing corruption in housing allocation, have been repeatedly targeted. As we will show later in this chapter, social movements have faced sustained campaigns of intimidation, violence, and assassination.

This violence is not random. It follows the fault lines of contestation: over land, housing, procurement, and political office. It punishes exposure and rewards silence. It is not the residue of a violent past. It is the architecture of the present. In place of the apartheid state's authoritarianism, we now face a decentralised but entrenched system of privatised coercion. The goal is not ideological domination, but control of resources and elimination of threats to corrupt power.

Tenderpreneurship — the use of political connections to secure state contracts — has flourished in this environment. Figures like Shauwn Mkhize, the Durban-based 'tenderpreneur' whose wealth stems from lucrative municipal contracts, illustrate how blurred the lines have become between business, politics, celebrity, and gangsterism. The assassination of construction industry rivals and the use of intimidation to secure contracts are often quietly tolerated or ignored.

The cumulative result is a system in which public resources are militarised. The awarding of a contract can trigger a killing. A councillor appointment can incite a gang war. A protest can provoke a police assassination. Violence becomes the means through which political and economic power is maintained.

This is not merely state failure. It is the emergence of a new kind of state — a state that kills not in the name of ideology, but in defence of extraction. A state in which the line between governance and gangsterism is no longer clear.

Political Repression

Political repression remains a persistent feature of South African society. Independent political organising, particularly among the poor, is often met with surveillance, harassment, violence, and sometimes assassination. Rather than building a democratic political culture rooted in civic participation and popular sovereignty, the post-apartheid state has repeatedly treated autonomous grassroots mobilisation as a threat to order.

Marikana remains the most brutal example of post-apartheid repression. On 16 August 2012, police opened fire on striking mineworkers at Lonmin platinum mine, killing 34 and wounding dozens more. The massacre, carried out in full view of the media, was a turning point in post-apartheid political consciousness. It shocked the world in much the same way that Sharpeville had in 1960. It made clear that the state was prepared to kill workers to defend corporate interests. The subsequent Farlam Commission of Inquiry did not result in senior political figures being held accountable, and to this day, there has been no justice for the victims. But the story of repression extends far beyond Marikana.

Since the early 2000s, grassroots organisations like the Western Cape Anti-Eviction Campaign and the Landless People's Movement (LPM) have been subject to intense police repression. Both movements emerged to defend the rights of poor communities facing evictions, service disconnections, and displacement. In 2004, several members of the LPM were arrested and detained without trial under apartheid-era legislation. The Western Cape Anti-Eviction Campaign faced repeated violent evictions and intimidation by local authorities. These early instances set the tone for how the state would respond to dissent from below.

This repression has come in waves. It has not been consistent or total, but it has repeatedly intensified in response to mass mobilisation. Many have been subject to assassination, police violence, and unlawful arrests, harassment, including arrests on fabricated charges.

This pattern of political repression has also extended into the education sector. During the 2015–2016 #FeesMustFall student uprisings, heavily armed police were deployed onto university campuses across the country. Students were tear-gassed, shot with rubber bullets, and arrested en masse. While students were demanding access to education and the transformation of universities, the state responded with a security crackdown. Many student leaders continue to face criminal records and legal proceedings to this day.

The tactics of repression are multifaceted. Surveillance of activists is widespread, particularly those linked to land, housing, and student struggles. Police often accompany municipal officials during evictions, using force to suppress resistance. Unlawful arrests are used to remove movement leaders from communities and disrupt organising. Torture in police custody remains common. According to rights monitors, this includes beatings, suffocation, and the use of electric shocks. Prisons, too, have been implicated in abuse, with inmates reporting systemic torture and degrading treatment. These tactics have been supplemented by prolonged and punitive bail conditions, drawn-out court processes, and the deliberate targeting of movement leaders through legal harassment.

Municipal governments also play an active role in repression. Local authorities frequently deploy Anti-Land Invasion Units and the Metro Police to destroy homes, prevent community meetings, and intimidate residents. These acts are often violent and are rarely subject to legal consequences. Municipal bylaws have been weaponised to curtail protest, informal trade, and public assembly — frequently targeting the poor under the guise of maintaining order.

Repression is not only enacted by the state, but also by actors connected to the ruling party. Local ANC officials have been repeatedly implicated in mobilising violence against activists. In some cases, gunmen linked to ANC networks have been involved in assassinations. This merging of party and state power with informal violence creates a highly dangerous environment for independent organising. Some NGOs and academics have also contributed to repression by misrepresenting and defaming movements that have refused to accept their authority.

The legal system itself is often used as an instrument of repression. Movement leaders are frequently subjected to arrest on baseless charges, and cases are repeatedly postponed, creating a form of punishment through process. Bail conditions are often punitive, restricting political activity and movement. Oversight mechanisms such as IPID have failed to hold police accountable, and intelligence agencies continue to monitor activists and infiltrate organisations.

Assassinations of grassroots environmental and land activists further illustrate the stakes of independent organising. Fikile Ntshangase, an anti-mining activist, was murdered in 2020 for her opposition to coal mining in KwaZulu-Natal. Sikhosiphi 'Bazooka' Radebe, a prominent opponent of titanium mining on the Wild Coast, was gunned down outside his home in 2016. These killings remain unresolved and highlight the extreme risks faced by those who challenge powerful interests. These assassinations also illustrate the intersection of corporate power, traditional authority, and political elites in South Africa's extractive economy — a nexus that shields itself from public scrutiny and accountability. Scholars such as Nomboniso Gasa have explored how this collusion creates an environment in which dissent is silenced to protect powerful interests.

This pattern of repression is not unique to South Africa. Across Latin America, social movements fighting for land, indigenous rights, and political accountability have faced systematic state violence. In countries like Brazil, Colombia, and Honduras, grassroots organisers have been harassed, criminalised, and assassinated. In many cases, states rely on militarised police, paramilitary groups, or legal persecution to suppress dissent. The parallels with South Africa underscore a global pattern in which the poor and those who organise independently are treated as threats to be managed rather than citizens to be engaged.

CHAPTER 7

Lessons from the International Left

The ANC's moral and organisational collapse has opened the door to new political forces, but what has emerged is not a democratic or emancipatory left. Instead, we have seen the rise of a fake left — parties like the Economic Freedom Fighters (EFF) and the uMkhonto weSizwe Party (MKP) that borrow the language of radical politics to serve deeply authoritarian, corrupt, and, in the case of the MKP, an ethnonationalist agenda. These formations are not in any meaningful sense part of a left tradition.

There is no genuine left in South Africa's electoral politics. The political parties that claim to speak for the poor and working class are often little more than vehicles for personal ambition or elite factionalism. They do not support popular struggles, they do not build rooted democratic organisations, and they do not present a coherent vision of transformation.

The trade unions have also failed to engage with this crisis meaningfully. They have not offered a broader political vision or sought to build solidarity across the wide spectrum of contemporary struggles. In many cases, there is a deep complicity between trade union leadership and the corrupt political elite that surrounds the ANC. A senior union leader is widely understood to be wholly captured by a donor. The response of unions to grassroots politics has often been marked by a class arrogance — mirroring the broader contempt that many in the middle class show towards the poor.

There are still living currents of the left in South Africa. Some intellectuals continue to speak and write with clarity and courage. There are forms of grassroots politics that offer a compelling alternative to the rot in electoral politics: built from below, committed to dignity, and clear and courageous in its opposition to authoritarianism, xenophobia, and corruption. But grassroots struggles have not developed an electoral project and remain largely outside the formal political arena.

This leaves us with a serious strategic question. If the genuine left is not in parliament, not leading the unions, and not able to contend for power, where is it? And what would it take to build it?

One place to look for answers is the international terrain. Across Latin America and in the Caribbean and the European south, movements and parties have built powerful, if uneven, projects rooted in the left traditions of dignity, solidarity, and popular power. Some have succeeded. Some have failed. Some are still unfolding. But all offer vital lessons for our time.

Haiti

Haiti was the site of the world's first successful slave revolution and the creation of the first Black republic. In

1804, after defeating French colonial forces, formerly enslaved people declared independence — and in doing so, shattered the global order of slavery and empire. That victory provoked immediate and enduring retaliation. Haiti was isolated diplomatically and economically and punished for its defiance. In 1825, France returned with warships to demand reparations for the 'loss' of its enslaved population and plantations — a debt that Haiti spent more than a century repaying, draining its resources and entrenching poverty. The country has been subject to repeated foreign interventions ever since.

In 1990, nearly two centuries after independence, Haiti elected its first truly democratic president: Jean-Bertrand Aristide. A former Catholic priest deeply shaped by liberation theology, Aristide was a vocal advocate for the poor and a leading figure in the Lavalas movement — a mass-based political project rooted in popular democracy, participatory organising, and the struggle for dignity. His campaign broke from the country's elite politics, drawing strength from the streets, churches, and urban and rural communities long excluded from power.

Aristide won a landslide victory, with nearly 70% of the vote. But only months into his presidency, he was overthrown in a military coup backed by the United States. He was forced into exile while his supporters were massacred, arrested, or driven into hiding. Though he was reinstated in 1994 under US supervision, his government was sharply constrained. Foreign donors and international institutions dictated economic policy. Elite resistance remained strong.

In 2000, Aristide won a second term with overwhelming support. His government launched literacy campaigns, school feeding schemes, a push to end child labour, and steps toward agrarian reform. But in 2004, amid growing pressure from armed groups and international actors, Aristide was again removed from power at gunpoint by US Marines. What followed was not only another unelected regime, but the effective dismantling of popular political life. Lavalas was banned from elections. UN troops occupied the country. Civil society was fragmented. A once-vibrant movement was forced underground.

The Haitian example contains urgent lessons. It shows that popular legitimacy is not a protection against imperialism. Even overwhelming electoral mandates can be overturned through pressure, coercion, or force — especially when the interests of the poor clash with those of entrenched elites and global powers. It also shows that popular movements need more than mass support: they need political strategies for survival, including anticipating repression and building transnational solidarity.

As Pithouse has noted in an important academic piece, the 2004 coup in Haiti was widely supported by white liberal opinion in South Africa, including by prominent figures such as former Democratic Alliance leader Tony Leon, as well as most of the liberal press. This is a sobering warning. It shows that much of the white liberal commentariat in South Africa is willing to align itself with imperialist projects when they seek to crush Black sovereignty and mass-based political alternatives. What happened in Haiti is not just a story about Haiti. It is a mirror, too — showing how elite consensus in other parts of the world, including South Africa, can be mobilised against emancipatory projects in the Global South.

There is another deeper lesson as well. Haiti has never been allowed to fully realise the promise of its revolution. Every attempt to do so — from 1804 to 2004 — has been met with containment. The country remains a laboratory of imperialism, a site where the limits of sovereignty in the Global South are repeatedly enforced. Any emancipatory project must grapple with this history — and with the reality that a victory at the ballot box does not end the power of empire.

Venezuela

The Bolivarian Revolution in Venezuela began with enormous hope. Hugo Chávez's 1998 election marked the rise of a popular, anti-neoliberal left that placed the working class and the poor at the centre of political life. Drawing on a long tradition of Latin American radicalism and inspired by the legacy of Simón Bolívar, Chávez's movement reasserted national sovereignty, challenged US hegemony, and undertook a major redistribution of resources.

The early achievements were significant: poverty dropped, education and healthcare were dramatically expanded, and Venezuela played a leadership role in building regional alliances like the *Alianza Bolivariana para los Pueblos de Nuestra América* (Alba). A key part of this vision was the *comuna* — a grassroots form of popular power that aimed to deepen democracy from below by giving communities direct control over land, services, and governance. These institutions represented the most promising and participatory element of the Bolivarian process.

But even during the Chávez years, the concentration of power in the presidency created structural weaknesses. The central state increasingly became the only meaningful vehicle for change. As a result, when that state faltered, so too did many of the revolutionary initiatives.

Under Chávez's successor, Nicolás Maduro, the problems deepened. The economic crisis triggered by falling oil prices was compounded by severe US sanctions aimed at collapsing the government. These sanctions must be clearly condemned. They have devastated ordinary Venezuelans, caused immense suffering, and constitute a form of collective punishment. But the collapse of the economy and the degeneration of public institutions cannot be explained by sanctions alone.

Maduro's administration has been marked by systemic corruption, growing authoritarianism, and the erosion of democratic norms. Independent left voices have been repressed, elections have been manipulated, and institutions hollowed out. Rather than empowering the communes and autonomous grassroots forces, the state increasingly sought to control or neutralise them. Corruption became deeply entrenched, undermining the credibility of the revolutionary process and contributing to the mass exodus of millions of Venezuelans.

There are two key lessons here for South Africa. First, meaningful transformation must go beyond the state. If the state becomes the sole custodian of change, it risks reproducing the very forms of exclusion it claims to oppose. The Bolivarian communes remain a powerful example of what democratic grassroots organisation can achieve — but they must be allowed to flourish independently of state and party control.

Second, corruption is not a side issue. It eats away at political legitimacy, destroys public trust, and creates the conditions in which authoritarianism thrives. A truly emancipatory politics cannot coexist with systemic theft and elite enrichment. Venezuela shows us that if popular energies are captured by a corrupt state, the results can be catastrophic.

At its best, Venezuela reminded the world that mass politics rooted in dignity and sovereignty is possible. But for those lessons to endure, the left must insist on democratic accountability, decentralised power, and a clear break with corruption — especially within its own ranks.

Bolivia

Bolivia under Evo Morales and the Movement Toward Socialism (MAS) was one of the most important achievements of the Latin American left in the 21st century. Morales became the country's first Indigenous president in 2006, following decades of militant struggle by trade unions, Indigenous organisations, and the urban poor. His rise was a direct challenge to centuries of colonial domination and neoliberal orthodoxy.

Under Morales, the MAS government delivered significant gains: nationalising gas and mining resources, reducing extreme poverty, expanding public education and healthcare, and affirming the plurinational identity of Bolivia. Indigenous culture, languages, and worldviews were brought into the heart of state discourse and symbolism. The 2009 constitution was a major moment of institutional innovation from below, recognising Bolivia as a plurinational state and enshrining collective rights.

Yet over time, power within the movement became increasingly centralised. Morales's style of leadership became more vertical and personalistic. Dissenting voices within the movement — including Indigenous feminists, environmentalists, and rural organisers — were marginalised. Civil society spaces were narrowed. In 2016, Morales lost a referendum on term limits. Rather than step aside, he turned to the courts to overturn the outcome and stood for a fourth term in 2019.

This decision opened the door for elite backlash. The 2019 election result was disputed by the US-funded Organisation of American States, which falsely claimed electoral fraud. These bogus claims were used to justify a military-backed coup that forced Morales into exile. The coup regime, led by Jeanine Áñez, unleashed deadly violence against Indigenous protesters, with massacres in Sacaba and Senkata. A US-aligned elite, with support from parts of the military, the Catholic Church, and right-wing Latin American governments, tried to reverse the gains of the MAS era through brute force.

In 2020, MAS returned to power through the ballot box. Luis Arce, a former finance minister under Morales, won a decisive victory, affirming that MAS retained broad popular support. But instead of strengthening the movement through internal renewal and unity, conflict quickly emerged. Morales returned from exile and reasserted himself as the true leader of MAS. Rather than support Arce's leadership from a distance, Morales attempted to control the party from within, sidelining Arce and accusing him of betrayal. Arce, in turn, attempted to assert independence, promote generational change, and reduce the personalist character of MAS politics.

This power struggle has fractured the movement. Morales has accused Arce and his allies of conspiring with the right and betraying the process of change. Arce's supporters have accused Morales of refusing to let go and trying to install loyalists regardless of public legitimacy. Local elections exposed deepening divisions, and in recent months the movement has split into rival factions — a dynamic that resulted in the electoral defeat of the left.

The Bolivian experience offers hard but essential lessons for the South African left. A movement rooted in popular struggle and capable of governing well must still guard against internal rot. Electoral success is not the same as movement democracy. Leadership cannot become permanent without consequence. If the political project remains hostage to one personality, it is vulnerable to both authoritarian tendencies from within and external attack. Renewal, decentralisation, and meaningful democracy from below are not luxuries — they are survival strategies.

Greece

In the wake of the 2008 global financial crisis, Greece became ground zero for a brutal experiment in austerity. The EU, European Central Bank, and IMF — often called the 'Troika' — imposed crushing conditions in exchange for bailouts. Public services were gutted, wages and pensions slashed, and unemployment soared. The social fabric of the country began to tear.

In July 2015, Syriza's government called a referendum asking the Greek people whether they accepted the latest round of bailout conditions. Over 61% voted 'No'. It was a moment of extraordinary democratic defiance. Yet within days, the government capitulated, signing an agreement even harsher than the one voters had rejected. The referendum was not just a policy choice — it was a mass democratic expression against technocratic rule, and its rejection marked one of the most glaring moments where the will of a people was discarded to appease capital.

After the capitulation, Syriza fractured. A left-wing breakaway faction, Popular Unity, attempted to reconstitute a more militant anti-austerity project but failed to gain traction. The speed with which Syriza lost coherence after 2015 points to a deeper organisational fragility — without grassroots institutions of power, disappointment quickly becomes demobilisation. Betrayal from above can rapidly demoralise a base and disorganise movement energy, especially if institutions of popular power — such as workers' councils or neighbourhood assemblies — have not been built.

Syriza's rise from social movements was meteoric — but short-lived. Its capitulation to the EU showed that without structural economic power, electoral victories can be hollowed out. Syriza showed that where debt and capital markets hold the leash, political power becomes largely symbolic. For countries in the Global South, the lesson is clear: without insulating democratic mandates from financial coercion, the left risks becoming a manager of misery.

Brazil

Brazil's contemporary left project is the result of decades of determined organising. The Workers' Party (PT), co-founded by Luiz Inácio Lula da Silva in 1980, grew out of the trade union movement, popular education initiatives, and liberation theology — an expression of faith rooted in the struggles of the poor. Lula himself was born into a large, impoverished family in rural Pernambuco and raised by a single mother. His father was an abusive alcoholic. Lula left school early, moved to the industrial periphery of São Paulo, and became a metalworker. His rise from factory floors to the presidency is emblematic of Brazil's social contradictions — and carries deep resonance for South Africans, where millions share similar stories of rural displacement, precarity, and survival.

After years of movement-building, Lula was elected in 2002 and took office in 2003. His government oversaw some of the most significant reductions in poverty and inequality in Brazilian history. Programmes like Bolsa Família, which provided conditional cash transfers to millions of poor households, were globally lauded. Investment in education, housing, and health expanded access and affirmed rights. These gains were accompanied by strong democratic legitimacy and popular mobilisation. The PT understood that redistributive governance had to be rooted in mass organisation — and it maintained strong ties with social movements such as the Landless Workers' Movement (MST) and urban housing campaigns.

The MST and the MTST (Homeless Workers' Movement) are among the most serious political actors in Brazil. They combine direct action — such as occupations of land or housing — with highly organised political education and the provision of material support to their members, including land, food, and housing. Both movements run political education schools and take the work of political formation seriously. This commitment to meeting people's needs while building political consciousness gives them deep roots in working-class communities.

In Brazil, as in much of Latin America, there are large numbers of university-trained intellectuals who work productively and constructively with social movements. Many draw on the ideas of Paulo Freire, whose vision of dialogical education remains influential. While South Africa has produced some deeply committed intellectuals who are trusted and respected by grassroots movements, in general, university-trained intellectuals either have no relationship to popular struggles or have tried to direct them from above, resulting in broken relationships and sometimes quite serious antagonism. There have been a number of cases where university-trained intellectuals have mounted serious and sometimes scurrilous attacks against the leaders of trade unions or grassroots movements who prefer to take instruction from their members rather than from above. This is a serious problem that needs to be addressed.

However, the Brazilian elite never accepted this transformation. A sustained backlash — judicial, parliamentary, and media-led — culminated in the 2016 soft coup against President Dilma Rousseff, Lula's successor. Lula himself was imprisoned on spurious charges, paving the way for the rise of the far-right under Jair Bolsonaro. The return of Lula to the presidency in 2023, after his exoneration, marks a stunning political reversal and shows the depth of the PT's institutional and social resilience.

Brazil's trajectory offers profound lessons for South Africa. Lula's journey — from rural poverty and violent hardship to labour organising and democratic leadership — resonates deeply with the lived experiences of millions of South Africans. But more than inspiration, Brazil offers a model of how to build a serious, long-term left project: one that is rooted in everyday struggles, anchored in moral clarity, and capable of transforming the state without being consumed by it. It shows that it is possible to hold together movements, institutions, and ideas in a shared struggle for dignity and redistribution — even in the face of violence, coups, and imperial hostility. In South Africa, the broader left remains fragmented and institutionally weak, and Brazil stands as a reminder that no shortcut can substitute for the hard work of organising, building alliances, and sustaining hope across decades.

Colombia

Colombia's 2022 election marked a historic turning point. For the first time, the country elected a leftist president, Gustavo Petro, a former guerrilla and long-time senator, alongside Francia Márquez, an Afro-

Colombian environmental and human rights activist who emerged from the grassroots struggles of the Pacific coast. Their victory broke the grip of a reactionary political order rooted in oligarchic power, paramilitarism, and US influence. It was a triumph born not from a single party or charismatic leader but from a broad coalition of movements, organisations, and political traditions united in the *Pacto Histórico* (Historic Pact).

The Petro–Márquez project did not emerge from a vacuum. It was the culmination of years of social struggle — from the student uprisings of 2011 and 2018, to Indigenous and Afro-Colombian resistance, to the massive 2021 national strike that paralysed the country. These mobilisations were not simply reactive; they articulated bold demands for a new society — feminist, ecological, anti-racist, and democratic. Márquez's campaign slogan, '*vivir sabroso*' (to live richly or with dignity), captured the spirit of this popular desire for a life beyond violence, poverty, and ecological destruction.

Petro's political trajectory embodies many of Colombia's central contradictions. Born in 1960 to a modest family on the Caribbean coast, he joined the leftist guerrilla movement M-19 as a young man, not to take up arms - he has often stressed - but to organise politically. He was arrested in 1985 and spent 18 months in prison, where he was reportedly tortured. After the demobilisation of M-19, Petro entered legal politics, eventually becoming a senator known for his investigations into paramilitary networks and corruption at the highest levels of government. His time as mayor of Bogotá (2012–2015) was marked by bold, redistributive policies and fierce institutional opposition.

Petro is a voracious reader with a strong interest in Marxism, liberation theology, and ecological economics. He speaks often of "overcoming the fossil fuel economy" and has tried to forge a democratic, ecological, and popular left — one that rejects both neoliberalism and authoritarianism. His long and difficult path to the presidency has given him a complex, layered political vision that resists easy categorisation.

Márquez, Petro's deputy, affirms the political agency of those long excluded: rural women, Afro-descendants, and environmental defenders. She speaks with clarity and force about the intersection of race, gender, and class — and insists on the value of collective life.

In many ways, the current project in Colombia represents a new kind of political imagination. Petro's administration includes feminists, Indigenous leaders, peace negotiators, and economists committed to ecological transition. Rather than imposing a singular ideological line, the Historic Pact is a strategic alliance across difference — one grounded in shared struggle, not elite consensus. The emphasis on care, justice, and sustainability as pillars of policy reflects a shift away from traditional left statism toward something more plural, intersectional, and democratic.

The Colombian left has a long and often tragic history. From the repression of the Patriotic Union in the 1980s to the decades-long armed conflict and the brutal targeting of trade unionists, social leaders, and community organisers, the price of left politics has been extraordinarily high. Entire generations have been disappeared or assassinated. That a democratic and plural left has been able to emerge from this context is a remarkable achievement — a testament to the courage and endurance of communities that never stopped organising. Petro and Márquez do not represent a sudden break with the past, but rather the political flowering of a long resistance.

This new project faces formidable obstacles. Colombia remains marked by paramilitary violence, the persistence of narco-politics, and deep economic inequality. Parts of the state and security apparatus are openly hostile to reform. The old oligarchy and the US foreign policy establishment continue to see any deviation from neoliberal orthodoxy as a threat. Yet despite these forces, the Petro–Márquez government has pushed forward reforms on tax justice, peace negotiations, labour rights, and land redistribution. While far from secure, the coalition has managed to maintain both mass support and institutional credibility.

Colombia under Petro has also played a growing international role. It has positioned itself alongside South Africa as one of the most outspoken governments in defence of Palestine — taking a principled stance against Israeli aggression and calling for accountability under international law. In Latin America, Petro has sought to rebuild regional solidarity, revive the idea of a united Latin American left, and reassert the autonomy of the region in the face of renewed US pressure.

For South Africa, where the left remains fragmented and often trapped in sterile ideological purism or NGO-driven technocracy, the Colombian example is instructive. It shows that a coalition of forces — including grassroots movements, former rebels, feminists, and progressive professionals — can come together not by erasing difference, but by organising through it. It affirms the possibility of building electoral power without abandoning struggle. And it offers a reminder that the most vital energy often comes not from established parties or prominent men, but from women, youth, and communities who have long borne the weight of exclusion and violence.

Colombia's emerging left has given new shape to the Latin American left — and to global conversations about how unity, imagination, and determination can challenge entrenched power.

Lessons for South Africa

Across the international left, transformative projects have won and lost, flourished and faltered. But each experience carries lessons for those seeking democratic transformation elsewhere.

The Haitian example makes clear that left governments will face intense opposition from entrenched elites and international forces. Even where there is deep and popular support, this pressure can result in violent destabilisation. The lesson is not that popular movements are a guarantee against defeat, but that they are a vital precondition for resilience. Left projects that lack a well-rooted mass base — as was the case in Greece — are vulnerable to being swiftly neutralised, even after dramatic electoral victories.

Bolivia's trajectory points to the dangers of personalism. When movements become too tightly tied to singular personalities, succession becomes fraught, and unity can fracture. Venezuela shows a similar risk: the communal experiments launched under Chávez were promising, but the consolidation of power under Maduro, amid worsening corruption and economic crisis, has undermined much of that early energy. The Brazilian experience, by contrast, underscores the importance of long-term organising, political education, and programme-based unity. Decades of patient work laid the groundwork for real redistributive reforms and institutional durability — even amid repression and reaction.

Colombia's case shows the potential of broad coalitions grounded in real struggle, and rooted in feminist, ecological, and anti-racist politics. It also highlights the importance of a clear break with both technocratic liberalism and authoritarian populism, and a willingness to forge strategic unity across diverse constituencies.

For South Africa, these examples suggest that building a viable left alternative will require long-term organising, political education, and the development of ethical, grassroots cadre. It also demands alliances between progressive lawyers, educators, and organisers who are willing to work under the leadership of communities. These roles must be played in support of, rather than in substitution for, mass political participation.

In countries that have built viable left formations, people have been able to work together across differences. In South Africa, by contrast, these linkages have been far weaker. The middle-class left is politically immature and intensely sectarian, often to the point of being extremely toxic. We need to build broad coalitions based on mutual respect.

In South Africa, there have, in many cases, been complete breakdowns between progressive movements and left intellectuals, as a result of the latter wishing to dominate grassroots struggles rather than to engage them on a dialogical basis. They have often tried to use donor money to ensure their domination.

The challenge ahead is formidable. But if we are to build a credible and principled left in South Africa — one that can offer a genuine alternative to repression, corruption, and despair — we must commit to democratic practices, shared learning, and patient institution-building from below. There are no shortcuts, but there is a wealth of experience to draw on.

CHAPTER 8

The South African left

South Africa urgently needs a viable, democratic left alternative. The current situation is a deepening crisis for the majority of people. Mass unemployment, systemic inequality, pervasive violence and decaying infrastructure have created a society marked by desperation, fear, and anger. For many, the promise of democracy has given way to a daily struggle for survival. In this context, the failure to construct a credible and principled left project has left a dangerous vacuum in the political landscape.

In the absence of such an alternative, authoritarian and right-wing forces have begun to fill the void. Parties such as ActionSA, the Patriotic Alliance, and MKP offer populist slogans and scapegoats but no meaningful solutions. They often draw on anti-democratic, xenophobic, or militarised impulses, and in some cases, operate through patronage networks that further entrench corruption. The risk is no longer abstract. If this trajectory continues, it is not inconceivable that South Africa's democratic experiment — fragile, uneven, and hard-won — could be brought to an end by the very forces now gaining ground.

There was a time when many on the left believed that the decline of the ANC would naturally give rise to something more progressive. That assumption has not held. While the ANC has indeed entered a phase of terminal decline, the most prominent new political formations to emerge are reactionary rather than emancipatory.

The Economic Freedom Fighters, though often described as left, offer a model rooted in authoritarianism, spectacle, and predatory politics. MKP is even more dangerous — a party shaped by a mix of deeply conservative, sometimes feudal and right-wing ideas, and militarism harnessed to an already predatory, violent and ethnically mediated form of politics in KwaZulu-Natal. The willingness of a publication like *The Guardian* to present these formations as 'left' is not just misleading — it is politically ignorant, and speaks to the global shallowness of contemporary liberal political discourse.

Alongside the rise of these authoritarian forces, a series of liberal parties — always well-funded by white capital — have also emerged, promising a new kind of politics. Formations like Mamphela Ramphele's Agang SA, Mmusi Maimane's Build One South Africa, and Songezo Zibi's Rise Mzansi have positioned themselves as technocratic and centrist alternatives. But despite slick campaigns and favourable media coverage, they have consistently failed at the polls.

These formations do not speak to the daily realities or political aspirations of most South Africans. Their base remains narrow, and their visions uninspiring. The political vacuum cannot be filled by donor-driven projects that mistake managerial competence for popular legitimacy. What is required is a credible left project: rooted in struggle, accountable to ordinary people, and serious about building democratic power from below.

A Historical Legacy: Three Pillars of the Anti-Apartheid Left

At the end of apartheid, there were three major left forces: the South African Communist Party (SACP), the Congress of South African Trade Unions (Cosatu), and the United Democratic Front (UDF). Each carried significant historical weight and mass support. But over the last three decades, all three have become politically marginalised — either through incorporation into the ANC-led alliance or through demobilisation.

The SACP, once a central intellectual contributor to the anti-apartheid movement, was rapidly absorbed into the elite nationalism of the ANC. Over time, its independence was lost as many of its leading figures took up positions in government. During Blade Nzimande's long tenure as general secretary, the party aligned itself to Zuma, supporting him through his rape trial and his bid for the presidency — a shameful betrayal of its historic commitments. Cosatu's former general secretary, Zwelinzima Vavi, too, supported Zuma at that time. The result was a deep loss of credibility.

In recent years, Nzimande has been removed as general secretary and replaced by Solly Mapaila. Some who had left the party during Nzimande's leadership have now returned, and new members have joined. The party maintains a large membership base and continues to provide political education. Many of its members have a relatively sophisticated understanding of imperialism and global politics. But structurally, it has functioned more as a mechanism to contain and control the left than to advance its goals independently.

Cosatu has also been co-opted. The trade union movement has deep roots in the democratic worker militancy of the 1973 Durban strikes. The Federation of South African Trade Unions (Fosatu), formed in 1979 and committed to worker control, was a key part of this legacy, and in 1985 it merged into Cosatu, which was launched in Durban as a major consolidation of independent, mass-based labour organisations. Initially, Cosatu offered a real challenge to capital and the state, often through grassroots participation and strike action.

But in post-apartheid South Africa, it has increasingly functioned as a support base for the ANC rather than an autonomous political actor. Many of its structures have become bureaucratised, and its leadership has frequently prioritised alliance discipline over worker interests. Its legitimacy has eroded, especially among younger and more precarious workers. The recent wave of independent worker organising — such as that seen among platform workers — reflects the extent of the vacuum left by Cosatu's retreat from militancy.

The UDF was the most important expression of popular democratic politics in the late apartheid era. It was launched in Cape Town in 1983 and rooted in a rich array of civic, religious, youth, cultural and labour organisations across the country. Its commitment to bottom-up organisation and its vision of a just and non-racial society made it a powerful and unifying force. Unlike the SACP and Cosatu, it was not incorporated into the ANC alliance, but it was effectively demobilised in the early 1990s. Still, its ethos remains a vital reference point for democratic struggles in South Africa.

As Neocosmos, the leading radical political theorist in South Africa, has argued, the UDF was not simply a set of organisations — it was a form of emancipatory politics grounded in the everyday practices and aspirations of ordinary people. Its orientation was not toward state power but toward building political subjectivities and horizontal solidarities. It emphasised the autonomy of popular politics, the dignity of ordinary people, and collective decision-making rooted in lived experience. The memory of the UDF experience does not offer a blueprint, but it does offer a vital connection to a still potent vision of politics in which the democratic power of ordinary people is both a means and an end of struggle.

The Left After Apartheid

There was a strong current in the South African left in the 1990s and early 2000s that abjured electoral politics. Influenced by global trends, many activists drew inspiration from texts like John Holloway's *Change the World Without Taking Power* and the work of Michael

Hardt and Antonio Negri, which were popularly interpreted to mean that the state could be bypassed altogether. This position was always fundamentally misguided. Meaningful and lasting transformation in any society requires engagement with the state, and that, in turn, necessitates an electoral project.

There have been two significant electoral experiments on the left since the end of apartheid, and a third is now on the horizon. The Workers and Socialist Party (WASP), a small Trotskyist sect, never managed to embed itself in actual struggles. Its dogmatic, sectarian approach and vanguardist orientation ensured its marginality from the start. Trotskyism was always a marginal force in South African political history, but in the post-apartheid period, it has come to dominate much of the left in NGO and academic spaces. The Trotskyist tactic of entryism — the strategy of infiltrating and attempting to take over mass-based organisations — has been especially destructive and has led to the collapse of numerous promising political projects.

The Socialist Revolutionary Workers Party (SRWP), launched by trade union Numsa, began with considerably more promise. It rapidly built a large membership base, and its founding conference in 2018 was vibrant and hopeful. According to numerous insiders, the project rapidly ground to a halt because its leader, Irvin Jim, insisted on micromanaging every aspect of the organisation while lacking the time to do so. No decisions could be taken without his approval, and the SRWP slowly collapsed under the weight of personal and bureaucratic inertia. Furthermore, like WASP, it failed to develop a political language grounded in the lived experiences of the people it sought to represent.

These failures illustrate the danger of launching electoral projects without the patient, foundational work of mass organising. They also show the limits of dogmatism. An effective left project must build internal democracy, avoid the stifling grip of personality cults, and develop a political language that enables ordinary people to both understand and shape it — a language rooted in lived realities, not abstract formulas.

The SACP has announced plans to contest the 2026 local government elections. It faces formidable obstacles. While the party retains a formal mass base, it has been largely absent from local struggles for years. If it fails to break with the top-down, dogmatic style that has characterised so many other failed attempts, it is highly unlikely to succeed. It is simply too dogmatic and alienated from ordinary people's everyday experiences.

Social movements after apartheid

In the early 2000s, a number of grassroots organisations emerged that sought to rebuild left politics outside the ANC alliance. These included the Anti-Privatisation Forum (APF) in Gauteng, the Western Cape Anti-Eviction Campaign, and the Landless People's Movement (LPM). The Western Cape Anti-Eviction Campaign was by far the most militant of these early formations, and marked an important shift away from NGO-led activism toward genuinely popular mobilisation.

The relationships between NGOs and the LPM were often complicated and contested, while the APF struggled with persistent internal sectarianism, which proved damaging. Despite these limitations, these organisations represented the first serious post-apartheid attempt to build a politics of the left grounded in community-based resistance and popular participation.

By the early 2000s, however, these formations had begun to collapse. Leadership conflicts, donor dependence, and internal divisions undermined their ability to sustain themselves. This fragmentation created a political vacuum — one that would soon be filled by a new wave of protests from below.

In 2004, a wave of township protests began to sweep across the country. Often dismissed as 'service delivery protests', these uprisings expressed a deeper rupture — the sense among millions that formal political freedom had not translated into material justice. Though largely unorganised at first, this rebellion of the poor marked a turning point: passive frustration gave way to collective defiance. The post-apartheid political order began to visibly crack under the weight of its own betrayals. Police repression intensified. At the same time, the space opened for new forms of political consciousness and organisation.

Some of the activists who had been involved in the APF, and some much smaller and more short-lived political projects such as the Concerned Citizens' Forum (CCF), were openly hostile to the emergence of new formations outside of their control. When Abahlali baseMjondolo emerged, it was met with suspicion and even hostility by certain figures who saw themselves as a vanguard. Some saw Abahlali's autonomy as a threat and actively sought to delegitimise the movement. In some cases, this took the form of the always destructive "rule it or ruin it" approach of sectarian politics. This was very clearly racialised, and unfortunately there has never been sufficient reflection on what happened on the part of certain actors.

Abahlali has since grown into the most significant grassroots movement in post-apartheid South Africa. Over nearly two decades, it has built a powerful and principled base rooted in the daily lives of poor and working-class people. With more than 180,000 paid-up members and over 100 branches, it is the largest movement of the urban poor in the country. It has developed its strength through political education, internal democracy, a refusal to be co-opted, and a fierce commitment to dignity.

Abahlali has consistently rejected alignment with political parties, including the ANC and SACP, and has insisted on autonomy as a precondition for real democracy. Its leaders are widely respected for their integrity, and the movement's political language speaks directly to lived experience in a way that has eluded both the sectarian left and elite political parties.

The movement has made tactical use of protest votes during waves of repression. This has been effective in dealing with repression, but it is not enough. The movement's key limitation is its ongoing — and frankly inexplicable — refusal to build an electoral project.

Trade Unions After Apartheid

The break between Numsa and the ANC-aligned union federation Cosatu marked another turning point. In 2013, at the behest of the SACP, Numsa was suspended and then formally expelled from Cosatu in 2014, after openly criticising both the ANC's neoliberal turn and the growing authoritarianism and corruption of Zuma's presidency. The union was independent of the ANC and critical of both neoliberalism and Zuma. Some academics excitedly spoke of a "Numsa moment" — but became embittered when they were not given influential roles in shaping the union's trajectory.

Numsa's expulsion represented a rupture of national significance and opened up a new political space in which militant and independent working-class politics could potentially be renewed. But that promise has not been realised.

In the aftermath of Numsa's expulsion, the South African Federation of Trade Unions (Saftu) was formally launched in 2017 as an independent alternative to Cosatu. Numsa is by far its largest and most powerful affiliate, and for a time it seemed that Saftu might offer a new national platform for militant unionism and left renewal.

But Saftu has struggled to fulfil that potential. Its organisational capacity is uneven, and its political effectiveness has been severely undermined by the complete breakdown in the relationship between Jim and Vavi. Vavi sees Jim as dogmatically Marxist and unwilling to build broad alliances. Jim, in turn, sees Vavi as captured by liberal NGOs.

Jim is widely understood to have been captured by an external benefactor who was, in the past, widely respected for supporting left organisations around the world in ways that respected their autonomy. However, following a leadership shift within the management of the donor's organisation during the Covid-19 period, this support has increasingly come with demands to shape political direction across movements in multiple countries. As a result, serious concerns have emerged about the role of the donor within the international left.

The breakdown between Jim and Vavi has left the federation in paralysis. Saftu has, in many ways, become a lame duck. Numsa remains militant on the shop floor and regularly wins gains for its members — but internally, nothing of consequence can happen without Jim's personal approval. Although he is an extraordinarily hardworking individual, this concentration of authority has often proved constraining. The political opportunity opened by Numsa's expulsion from Cosatu has not yet been realised. The left remains fragmented — and still lacks an electoral vehicle.

Prospects for Left Renewal

Perhaps the most damaging failure of the South African left has been the absence of a shared vision capable of uniting its diverse elements. In contexts where viable and transformative left projects have emerged, such as in Haiti and across Latin America, unity has often been patiently constructed across unions, popular movements, churches, Indigenous and Black movements, and sections of the professional middle class. This has not happened in South Africa. Instead, activists, intellectuals, and trade unionists have often worked in fragmented ways, with little attempt to forge a collective political direction.

Another major weakness has been the idea that NGOs could substitute for popular movements. While some NGOs have played supportive roles, they cannot replace mass-based organising. Popular movements grounded in struggle and accountable to their members are irreplaceable. Nor can serious left projects be built purely through technocratic interventions, donor projects, or policy workshops. A viable left must emerge from real grassroots organising and be sustained through political education, democratic practice, and shared struggle.

There has also been an assumption, common in both academic and donor spaces, that intellectuals — often middle-class professionals — should provide political direction for popular organisations. This has contributed to the widespread breakdown in relationships between movements and left intellectuals. Too often, intellectuals have sought to dominate rather than collaborate. Rather than recognising that theory is also produced within struggle, they have treated movements as laboratories for their ideas or vehicles for their careers. Attempts to use donor money to exercise control over organisations have further poisoned these relationships.

At the same time, it must be acknowledged that careerism and opportunism are not limited to the middle class. Many grassroots activists have also oriented themselves around access to donor funds or political office, and there have been a number of cases of corruption. Xolani Klaas from the Social Justice Coalition, who was expelled from the organisation after being found guilty of corruption, is a well-known example. The result has been a general erosion of ethical seriousness. If a new left is to be built, it will require a real shift in political culture — one that affirms integrity, internal democracy, and accountability rather than personalised power, gatekeeping, or instrumentalism.

The role of progressive Christian traditions in the history of South African resistance cannot be overstated. During the anti-apartheid struggle, church-based organisations and figures — from the South African Council of Churches to leaders like Desmond Tutu and Beyers Naudé — played a crucial role in supporting grassroots organising, offering protection to activists, and providing an ethical language that linked material justice to moral responsibility. In many communities, churches served as vital organising hubs when political activity was banned or repressed. Today, however, the church is largely absent from left formations and popular movements. The vacuum left by its retreat from public life has narrowed the moral and institutional base of the democratic left. While some progressive clergy and faith-based organisations remain active, there has been no systematic attempt to rebuild links between contemporary movements and religious networks. This is a missed opportunity, especially given that the majority of South Africans continue to identify with faith-based worldviews. Any serious effort to build a broad front for justice should consider how to engage ethically and politically with progressive currents within religious institutions — not to instrumentalise them, but to build deeper solidarities grounded in shared commitments to human dignity and the collective good.

Political education should be a cornerstone of left renewal, understood not as indoctrination but as a dialogical process grounded in shared experience and mutual respect. The experience of the MST in Brazil is instructive here. The movement's political school has been an extraordinary example of participatory education rooted in movement practice. Abahlali baseMjondolo's participation in this school has been a valuable contribution to South–South learning. For South Africa, the task is to build similarly grounded institutions of political education — controlled by movements, not NGOs, and consciously anti-sectarian. Crucially, this education must be conducted in the languages people best understand. The NGO sector's attempts at political education have largely been ineffective, often experienced as patronising and detached from lived reality.

The problems with NGOs do not mean that movement spaces do not have their own issues. A common problem is the deeply entrenched political culture in South Africa in which crude sloganeering is mistaken for political clarity. In too many spaces, nuance and real thought are dismissed as betrayal or hesitation, and complexity is reduced to tired slogans. This kind of rhetorical militancy may appeal in moments of anger or urgency, but it offers no meaningful guidance for strategy or action. A serious left project requires the ability to think with care and subtlety, to grapple honestly with contradictions, and to speak to people's real experiences — not simply to recite pre-existing dogmas. Political clarity is not achieved by shouting louder, but by listening more deeply and thinking more rigorously.

One of the deepest challenges within the South African left is the persistence of sectarianism and a toxic political culture. There is a long-standing tendency to treat those outside of one's group with suspicion, contempt, or open hostility. Political disagreements are frequently personalised. This has not only fractured attempts to build broad fronts, but also demobilised people who might otherwise have become part of a new project. The 'rule it or ruin it' ethos — typical of sectarianism — has done immense damage.

Another serious problem is the general machismo that pervades the left. While this is particularly entrenched in the trade union movement, it also appears in other spaces. Abahlali baseMjondolo has been a notable exception, creating space for women to lead and contribute on an equal footing. But across much of the left, projects led by women are undervalued or sidelined. This gendered power dynamic is a major barrier to building a more inclusive and effective left.

Likewise, there is a widespread tendency among union and NGO actors to look down on the urban poor. This is both politically short-sighted and historically ignorant. In many parts of the world where the left has been a serious force — such as in Haiti and across Latin America — the urban poor have been central actors in transformative struggles. In South Africa, they are too often treated with paternalism or contempt.

What is needed is the development of a new layer of principled grassroots activists, radical professionals, and intellectuals committed to democratic practice and the support — not control — of popular organisations. Only through this kind of commitment can the South African left begin to rebuild with seriousness and hope.

CHAPTER 9

What the future holds

South Africa is a beautiful, heartbreaking country — as full of hope as it is of despair. Our people carry deep wounds, yet we are capable of extraordinary things. At the grassroots level, the courage of many of our best activists has been remarkable. At the level of the state, our case at the International Court of Justice against Israel's genocide of Palestinians shows the very best of us. And in sport, the Springboks' dominance in world rugby reminds us that when we act with collective purpose, we can meet the highest standards anywhere.

Today, our country stands at a crossroads defined by profound contradictions. The formal institutions of democracy remain intact, but their capacity to serve the public good has been steadily eroded. Corruption, factionalism, and patronage have hollowed out large parts of the state. Violence — from organised crime and political assassinations to everyday insecurity — has become a defining feature of public life. The moral authority once claimed by the governing party has been squandered through complicity with neoliberal orthodoxy, crony enrichment, and the neglect of the poor.

The result is a society where the promise of freedom coexists with deepening inequality and growing despair. Collapsing infrastructure, a failing healthcare system, and rampant unemployment have eroded faith in democracy itself. Confronting this reality requires a sober recognition of the scale of the crisis and a refusal to accept false choices between a failed status quo and reactionary alternatives. It also demands the construction of a new left political force — one capable of confronting entrenched power, renewing democratic life, and placing the needs of the majority at the centre of politics.

The current landscape of electoral politics is fragmented and volatile. No party commands an outright majority, and coalitions — often unstable, opportunistic, and driven by access to resources rather than shared principle — have become the norm. Governance has been treated as a route to personal enrichment rather than public service.

Since 1994, politics have crystallised around two blocs, each now in deep crisis. The first is the ANC and its offshoots, the Economic Freedom Fighters (EFF) and the uMkhonto weSizwe Party (MKP). All three invoke the language of liberation but practise authoritarian, personality-driven, and corrupt politics that betray its ideals. Each reproduces a militarised political culture in which spectacle substitutes for democratic deliberation, and resentment displaces hope.

The second bloc is the liberal formation, dominated by the Democratic Alliance and joined by newer projects such as Rise Mzansi and Build One South Africa. These parties, heavily backed by corporate capital, speak primarily to middle- and upper-class concerns. The DA remains rooted in a white liberal worldview, reflexively aligned with Western interests and unwilling to confront the racial character of its leadership and politics. Its technocratic liberalism promises efficiency without justice and governance without transformation. The newer liberal projects orbiting around it — Black-led but funded by white billionaires — enjoy fawning media coverage yet have failed to gain popular traction.

The third rising force is the reactionary populist right, grounded in xenophobia. Parties such as the Patriotic Alliance and ActionSA channel public disillusionment through scapegoating. Their leaders speak the language of toughness and order but offer only division and resentment. These forces have already converged with explicitly fascist movements such as Operation Dudula, whose street campaigns against migrants have normalised hatred and violence in public life. This is the classic pattern of democratic decay: demagogues rise amid inequality, despair, and corruption.

Alongside these blocs, numerous smaller parties — some ethnic or religious, others built around individuals — have proliferated. Voter participation continues to decline, reflecting widespread disillusionment. The overall picture is one of fragmentation and cynicism: the liberation movement hollowed out, the liberal centre insulated, and the right increasingly dangerous.

The rise of authoritarian and xenophobic politics has been normalised in the mainstream. State actors and sections of the media have lent legitimacy to this shift: the SABC has called Operation Dudula a "civic organisation", while other outlets describe it as "civil society" — obscuring its fascist nature. Over the last decade, Dudula has brought an organised, street-level dimension to xenophobic mobilisation, targeting mostly African and Asian migrants. Cloaked in patriotism, it raids shops, bars hospital access, and terrorises working-class neighbourhoods.

The danger lies not only in street violence but also in the adoption of its rhetoric by politicians across the spectrum. As in parts of Europe, South Asia, and Latin America, economic crisis, political opportunism, and strongman appeal are converging. In South Africa, xenophobia has become a cheap substitute for redistributive politics, channelling anger toward the vulnerable instead of the powerful.

Globally, far-right movements have learned to turn legitimate grievances — job losses, collapsing services, insecurity — into repressive projects. The fascist playbook thrives in despair: finding enemies, stoking fear, and presenting authoritarianism as order. Confronting this turn requires a principled, unapologetic left that rejects scapegoating, insists on the indivisibility of rights, and identifies the true adversaries — the structures of exploitation and corruption, not the poor.

The historic left formations that once anchored working-class politics have been severely weakened. The trade union movement, once capable of paralysing the apartheid state, has been eroded by deindustrialisation, casualisation, and bureaucratisation. Cosatu's incorporation into the ANC-led alliance blunted its independence. Numsa, expelled in 2013 for its criticism of Zuma, retains strong shop-floor power but is hampered by donor capture, factionalism, and a fixation on traditional industrial work that limits engagement with the new precarious economy.

The South African Communist Party, once the intellectual vanguard of the liberation movement, has become a loyal appendage of the ANC. Its claim that alliance participation enables progressive influence has lost credibility as neoliberalism deepens and inequality worsens. The party is almost entirely absent from grassroots struggle.

The Treatment Action Campaign, once a model of effective mobilisation linking law and mass action, has faded from the political landscape. Abahlali baseMjondolo, by contrast, remains a powerful grassroots force. Despite assassinations, arrests, and harassment, it has sustained and expanded its base and was the only significant organisation to challenge Operation Dudula directly. The trade unions and the SACP failed to do so — a telling measure of their retreat.

The middle-class left in universities and NGOs has often been paralysed by sectarianism. Petty rivalries and personal vendettas have displaced strategic unity. Some actors have even tried to destroy movements they could not control. This has alienated potential allies and discredited the intellectual left in the eyes of grassroots organisers.

Donor-funded NGOs, even when well-intentioned, frequently capture rather than strengthen movements.

While some, like the Socio-Economic Rights Institute, have played constructive roles, many have subordinated popular struggles to donor priorities. Activists are absorbed into salaried posts, decision-making is reshaped to suit funders, and dissent risks the loss of resources. The result is a depoliticised activism that manages rather than transforms.

International experience shows that this is not inevitable. In Latin America, broad coalitions have united unions, rural and urban struggles, feminists, and Indigenous movements to contest state power while maintaining autonomy. In parts of Europe, municipalist projects have shown that grassroots-based politics can win local power without losing accountability. These examples, despite their contradictions, demonstrate that it is possible to bridge sectors, sustain mobilisation, and link struggle to governance.

In South Africa, the absence of a comparable unifying instrument has left struggles of the poor and working class vulnerable to isolation and reversal. Gains in one area — a wage victory, a land occupation, a court win — are quickly undone elsewhere by capital or the state. Without mechanisms to connect these fronts, the left remains reactive, fragmented, and unable to set the national agenda.

Building a Left Party

Salar Mohandesi argues that the party should be understood not as a fixed apparatus designed solely to "take power" but as an articulator: an organisation that can link diverse social forces, sustain them through time, and develop a shared political content rooted in their own experiences. This rejects both the fetish of spontaneity and the illusion that political clarity can simply be injected from above. Unity emerges through sustained, embedded participation in multiple sites of struggle, and any electoral work must remain subordinate to building durable, extra-parliamentary forms of counter-power.

James Schneider's argument that a party must simultaneously build popular unity, popular power, and a popular alternative also has direct implications for how to avoid failure. Popular unity means forging alliances between core constituencies without one dominating the others; popular power means building institutions that can legislate and act from below; and a popular alternative means having a credible, lived vision for how society could be reorganised. Each of these requires a breadth of participation that resists both sectarianism and entryism.

Past attempts to build left parties in South Africa offer sobering lessons. The Trotskyist Workers and Socialist Party (WASP) contested the 2014 national and provincial elections but won no seats and quickly faded from the political scene. The Socialist Revolutionary

Workers Party (SRWP) was quite different from the tiny Trotskyist sect in that it was launched with the backing of Numsa, the country's largest trade union. But it suffered a similar fate in the 2019 elections, failing to secure representation despite significant organisational resources. These failures show that left rhetoric, formal structures, and even union support are not enough. Without deep roots in grassroots struggles, a clear unifying programme, and a language that resonates with ordinary people, a party will not succeed.

Avoiding donor and NGO capture is not just a matter of refusing certain kinds of funding; it is about building an independent material base so that strategic direction flows from members and communities rather than from external actors. If a party depends on donors to keep the lights on, it will inevitably face pressure to soften its challenges to the powerful. Here, Mohandesi's insistence on the party's autonomy from any single institutional or class fraction is critical. This autonomy must be matched by internal democratic structures that can withstand factional conflict without paralysing the organisation — a culture where disagreement is resolved through collective deliberation rather than through 'rule it or ruin it' brinkmanship.

This role for the party has several dimensions. First, it requires a political practice grounded in listening. Movements are not mere constituencies to be represented; they are living sources of analysis and strategy. The experience of a housing activist facing eviction, or a nurse working in a collapsing public hospital, should inform political direction, not simply illustrate it.

Second, it involves weaving together demands. Struggles often focus on immediate needs, but a party can link them into a larger vision, build solidarity across sectors, and develop strategies to contest power locally, provincially, and nationally.

Third, it must defend gains and movements. Where repression strikes, such a party could mobilise legal resources, public pressure, and direct support to protect activists and sustain organising through moments of defeat or exhaustion.

The organisational form matters. Such a party would need deep democracy, not only in its constitution but in daily life. Decision-making should be collective, transparent, and oriented towards building the capacity and confidence of the base. Political education should be integral, ensuring leadership renewal and preventing the accumulation of unaccountable power.

Discipline should shield the organisation from opportunism and destructive factionalism without replicating authoritarian habits. It would also need to keep at bay the notoriously toxic sectarian elements that have, in too many instances, derailed promising initiatives on the left — ensuring that the culture of the organisation encourages principled disagreement without descending into destructive infighting.

Unity would not be assumed in advance. It would be built through shared practice by linking diverse struggles into a coherent political project that is stronger than the sum of its parts. This requires an organisation that is embedded in, and accountable to, the movements from which it draws strength, and that is capable of engaging on multiple fronts: political, social, and ideological. As Mohandesi argues, the party's purpose is not to govern in place of the people but to help weave together the organisational fabric through which people can govern themselves.

The aim is not to construct an electoral machine that measures success only by seats won, nor a narrow cadre group closed off from broader participation. It is to create a political home where movements can find protection, strategic connection, and the ability to act at scale without losing their autonomy. Such a formation would work both within institutions and in the streets, resisting the pull towards either parliamentary routine or sporadic, spectacular confrontation.

It would think in decades rather than electoral cycles, building solidarity across divisions of race, gender, and geography, and challenging the entrenched "common sense" that privatisation is inevitable, that the poor must wait for the economy to grow before their needs are met, or that liberation was achieved once and for all in 1994.

In South Africa, this horizon means engaging with the unfinished work of the liberation struggle: land redistribution, economic democracy, decommodified access to basic services, and the dismantling of structures that reproduce racial and class domination. It means learning from the ANC's over-centralisation, its accommodation with capital, and its tolerance of corruption, without falling back into liberal parliamentarism or technocratic NGO politics.

It means weaving together the housing activist in Durban, the mineworker in Rustenburg, the rural organiser in Limpopo, and the climate campaigner in Cape Town into a single political project that understands these fights not as separate issues but as interconnected fronts in a shared struggle for dignity and ecological survival.

The work of building such a party cannot be outsourced to dogmatic political sects or NGOs. It can only emerge from the self-activity of working class and poor people, given organisational form and strategic clarity capable of withstanding the inevitable backlash from those whose wealth and power rest on the existing order. In this sense, a unifying political home is not a luxury but a necessity — the means by which movements can persist, connect, and advance in a hostile political landscape.

A new left party in South Africa must emerge in a hostile political environment, shaped by repression, elite power, and a long history of internal failures on the left. To survive, it cannot simply aspire to be "better" — it must embed, from its inception, the kinds of structures, cultures, and strategic habits that actively inoculate it against the familiar traps that have derailed promising projects in the past.

Charismatic leadership is not inherently a problem — movements often need figures who can communicate vision and inspire confidence. But in the absence of robust mechanisms for accountability and leadership renewal, charisma can slide into personalism. Schneider warns that without distributed, participatory forms of power, political projects become overly dependent on moments and personalities, leaving them brittle and unable to recover from setbacks.

Resisting nationalist chauvinism and xenophobia must be a foundational principle. In today's South Africa, where even mainstream parties have normalised scapegoating migrants, principled internationalism is a practical necessity to hold together a multi-ethnic working class. This is not an "add-on" to the party's programme — it is essential to building the solidarity that makes collective action possible.

Building a viable left party in South Africa will require learning from both successes and failures elsewhere — and applying those lessons to our own unique conditions. The point is not to imitate foreign models, but to adapt strategies and organisational principles that have worked in different contexts while guarding against their pitfalls.

One of the strongest lessons comes from Latin America, particularly Bolivia's Movement for Socialism (MAS) and Brazil's Workers' Party (PT). Both movements grew out of decades of grassroots work in trade unions, peasant federations, and neighbourhood committees before ever contesting national elections. This deep anchoring meant that when they did achieve state power, they were backed by real social forces outside parliament — capable of defending gains and holding leaders to account. For South Africa, the parallel is clear: a new left party cannot be an electoral shortcut; it must be the political expression of years of embedded organising in workplaces, informal settlements, rural areas, and community struggles.

The contrasting experience of Venezuela shows the danger of over-centralisation and excessive reliance on charismatic leadership: initial gains can quickly erode if political vitality is concentrated in the state rather than spread across autonomous social formations.

Another set of lessons emerges from Spain's municipalist movements. In cities like Barcelona and Madrid, grassroots platforms used participatory governance and decentralised decision-making to channel citizen energy into institutional politics without suffocating it. Neighbourhood assemblies fed directly into citywide policy, ensuring that elected representatives were continually accountable to their base.

This institutional creativity helped them avoid the stagnation that often follows electoral victories. Yet, similar projects in other European cities collapsed when electoral success led to detachment from movement life. For South Africa, this underlines the need for any institutional gains to be hardwired to active, local decision-making bodies that can keep political representatives grounded in popular priorities.

African histories offer both inspiration and caution. The early years of the PAIGC in Guinea-Bissau under Cabral demonstrated the possibility of uniting diverse communities — peasants, workers, intellectuals — in a disciplined, principled liberation movement. Cabral's insistence on humility in leadership, especially for cadres from more privileged backgrounds, is vital for the South African context, where class and educational divides often undermine unity on the left.

He argued that leadership should not elevate itself above the people but integrate with them, learning as much as it teaches. Just as importantly, Cabral viewed culture as a weapon of liberation — the daily practices, values, and collective memory that sustain resistance. For a new South African left party, this means nurturing a culture of dignity, solidarity, and public morality alongside political organising, ensuring that liberation is lived, not only legislated.

The dangers are equally instructive. Across the continent, many post-liberation movements ossified into ruling parties that were gradually absorbed into the state, lost their democratic vitality, and succumbed to authoritarian drift. These failures warn us that even principled movements must constantly renew themselves, remain rooted in their base, and avoid the temptations of state patronage.

There are also lessons to be drawn from South Africa's own recent history. As the only mass movement built after apartheid fell, Abahlali baseMjondolo has shown how sustained organising among the poor can produce both resilience and political clarity. Its vision is also internationalist, and its relationship with Brazil's MST is a rare example of genuine, horizontal solidarity between movements. Organisers have travelled between the two countries, exchanging strategies for land occupation, community self-organisation, and political education.

Abahlali has adapted MST's practices such as collective farming, commune-building, and the cultural-political ritual of mística to the urban shack settlement context. This has strengthened its organisational capacity and reinforced its political autonomy in the face of donor pressure. Crucially, this was achieved without NGO mediation, proving that direct movement-to-movement solidarity can bypass the distortions of professionalised activism and foster genuine mutual learning.

The Abahlali–MST relationship points to a broader strategic possibility: building an international network of movements in the Global South that share resources, develop political education together, and stand in solidarity when one of them comes under attack. In a world where authoritarianism and neoliberalism cross borders with ease, so too must solidarity and shared resistance.

Taken together, these experiences suggest that the path forward for a new South African left party is not to import a ready-made model, but to weave together the lessons of mass-based endurance, participatory governance, principled coalition-building, and genuine international solidarity between movements. This weaving must be grounded in humility of leadership, a living political culture, and the constant renewal of ties between party structures and the grassroots struggles that give them life.

The conditions for building a new left party will never be ideal. Waiting for the "right moment" risks letting the current political vacuum harden into something far more dangerous: an entrenched politics of authoritarianism, xenophobia, and elite neoliberalism. With electoral participation rates at historic lows (over 11 million registered voters did not cast ballots in the 2024 polls) and vast swathes of the population disengaged from formal politics, the task is not simply to prepare for the next election — it is to begin rebuilding political life from the ground up.

That rebuilding must start with trust. In a landscape marked by fragmentation, sectarianism, and past betrayals, no amount of manifesto writing can substitute for the slow, patient work of re-establishing relationships between unions, community organisations, rural movements, climate justice activists, feminist networks, and progressive faith-based groups. This is not a call for vague "unity," but for practical, jointly undertaken projects — campaigns for housing and against evictions, for clean water, and for the release of political prisoners — that allow fractured forces to act together and measure one another by deeds rather than rhetoric.

Political education will be a cornerstone from the outset. This cannot be reduced to occasional workshops or the distribution of reading materials. It should be a living process embedded in struggles.

From the beginning, the new party must weave its core values into everyday organising. Decades of neoliberal atomisation and political gangsterism have eroded public trust, making it essential to show in practice what dignity, mutual aid, honesty, and solidarity look like. These values must guide how meetings are run, how decisions are taken, how resources are shared, and how victories are celebrated. A political formation that lives these values will inspire far more confidence than one that simply proclaims them in speeches.

The foundations must also be laid with the certainty that repression and co-option will come. Leaders and organisers should be prepared for harassment, surveillance, and offers of personal advancement designed to fracture the project. From the outset, the new formation will need internal systems for legal defence, rapid solidarity mobilisation, and transparent accountability processes to address misconduct without handing the state or rival factions an easy pretext for disruption.

If this preparatory work begins now, it will not simply create the scaffolding for a future party; it will begin to shift the balance of forces in the present. Each alliance forged, each new cadre trained, each campaign won or defended will help to make the idea of a principled, democratic, mass-based left party less an aspiration and more a lived reality. In a moment when so many have lost faith in politics altogether, that lived reality will be the most compelling argument that another future is possible.

South Africa is in a decisive moment. The political settlement of 1994 ended formal apartheid but left the deep structures of racial capitalism largely untouched. Three decades later, the governing party's moral authority has collapsed under corruption, factionalism, and neoliberal accommodation. The opposition offers no credible path to transformation, and voter registration and turnout have sunk to historic lows.

A viable, principled, mass-based left alternative is a necessity for the survival of democratic life. Without it, public institutions will continue to hollow out, communities will be set against one another, and political power will remain in the hands of those who profit from inequality and division.

The work ahead demands humility in leadership, deep anchoring in working class and poor communities, and a political culture rooted in dignity and solidarity. It requires resisting donor and NGO capture, rejecting sectarianism, and refusing the lure of elite co-option. It means standing firm against nationalist chauvinism and scapegoating, even when such positions are unpopular with the mainstream media and online mobs.

What must begin now is the patient, deliberate work of building trust between fractured movements, political education rooted in lived struggle, alliances tested in joint action, and spaces where political life is renewed from below. This fight is unfolding now — in workplaces, shack settlements, rural villages, campuses, and neighbourhood committees.

If we act with clarity and solidarity, we can still shape a politics that serves the people rather than the powerful. The responsibility is ours — to build the democratic left project that these times demand and to carry it forward with the determination and imagination worthy of the struggles that came before us.

However, the necessity for an effective left party must be understood within the political terrain that actually exists rather than the one we might wish for. Over the past three decades, electoral politics have hardened around two dominant blocs that are both deeply compromised. Around them, new formations have emerged — some claiming to renew the promise of liberation, others offering liberal or technocratic alternatives, and still others turning sharply to the right.

Any serious effort to build a principled left project must reckon with this terrain. The creation of a mass-based democratic left party is essential for the long-term renewal of democracy, but it faces formidable barriers in the short term: the enormous financial demands of electoral politics, the concentration of media power, and the fragmentation of progressive forces. These realities mean that it could take a decade, or even a generation, to build a viable left party.

In the meantime, we cannot abandon the country to the authoritarian kleptocrats who, given the chance, would undo our democracy and institute a deeply corrupt dictatorship. We also cannot accept that the Democratic Alliance and its ilk are the only alternative to the authoritarian kleptocrats.

There must, in the short term, also be a social-democratic possibility — an alliance that brings together the non-corrupt and reform-minded elements within the ANC, liberals willing to move beyond the narrow racial and sometimes racist worldviews that have come to be associated with the Democratic Alliance, organised labour, and grassroots organisations. Such a coalition would not replace the work of building a democratic left, but it could open a path toward stability, modest reform, and moral renewal while that longer project continues.

For such a project to take shape, it would need to recover the idea that politics can serve the common good. South Africa's crisis is not only economic but moral — a collapse of trust, integrity, and public purpose. A social-democratic option could begin to restore faith in public life by placing redistribution, job creation, and accountable governance at its centre.

The redistribution it could achieve would be moderate rather than radical, but it would nonetheless be significant — strengthening public services, reducing inequality, and making the country more liveable for millions. It would recognise that economic growth and social justice are not opposing goals but interdependent: there can be no sustainable economy without dignity, education, healthcare, and decent work for the majority.

This possibility would depend on pragmatic alliances rather than ideological purity. Non-corrupt elements in the ANC still command electoral legitimacy in many communities, and despite rapid de-industrialisation and the collapse of some of the public-sector unions into mafias, sections of organised labour retain structures capable of mobilising collective power.

Elements within business are also coming to recognise that unending instability and deep inequality are incompatible with sustained investment. If such forces could agree on a common minimum programme — rebuilding the state, protecting public institutions, reversing de-industrialisation, investing in social infrastructure, and restoring ethical leadership — the country could be pulled back from the brink.

The greatest challenge would be credibility. After three decades of failure and betrayal, the public will not easily trust another elite-led project. Any social-democratic formation would have to demonstrate integrity not through rhetoric but through conduct: transparent funding, internal democracy, and the visible inclusion of trade unions and grassroots organisations. It would also have to break decisively with the xenophobic currents that corrode public life.

Such a project would not fulfil the hopes for more profound forms of change, but it could create the political and institutional breathing space in which that longer project might take root. The lesson of recent history — from Latin America to southern Europe — is that even modest reform coalitions can defend democracy and ease the social crisis when authoritarianism threatens to overwhelm it. In South Africa, a viable social-democratic bloc could stabilise the political system, reassert the principle that public office is a form of service, and reopen the horizon of hope.

South Africa is in crisis, but it has been in worse situations before and has found a way out. Today, we face a new moment of peril and must find an exit point into a better and more hopeful future.

www.ingramcontent.com/pod-product-compliance
Lightning Source LLC
Chambersburg PA
CBHW070328270326
41926CB00017B/3803